GOD'S CONSTANT PRESENCE

True Stories of Everyday Miracles

Embraced *by* His Light

GOD'S CONSTANT PRESENCE
True Stories of Everyday Miracles

Embraced *by* His Light

EDITORS OF GUIDEPOSTS

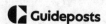

A Gift from Guideposts

Thank you for your purchase! We appreciate your support and want to express our gratitude with a special gift just for you.

Dive into *Spirit Lifters*, a complimentary booklet that will fortify your faith and offer solace during challenging moments. It contains 31 carefully selected verses from scripture that will soothe your soul and uplift your spirit.

Please use the QR code or go to **guideposts.org/spiritlifters** to download.

Embraced by His Light

Published by Guideposts
100 Reserve Road, Suite E200
Danbury, CT 06810
Guideposts.org

Copyright © 2024 by Guideposts. All rights reserved.
This book, or parts thereof, may not be reproduced, stored in a retrieval system, or transmitted in any form or by any means, electronic, mechanical, photocopying, recording or otherwise, without the written permission of the publisher.

Cover design by Serena Fox Design Company
Interior design by Serena Fox Design Company
Cover photo by Shutterstock
Typeset by Aptara, Inc.

ISBN 978-1-961126-39-8 (hardcover)
ISBN 978-1-961251-74-8 (softcover)
ISBN 978-1-961126-40-4 (epub)

Printed and bound in the United States of America
10 9 8 7 6 5 4 3 2 1

> God's word is a lamp, but not a flood lamp. More like a flashlight. . . . God's word illuminates one step at a time because that's all we really need to see and know.
>
> —*Tracy Wilde-Pace*

TABLE *of* CONTENTS

Introduction 4
  For the Glory of God

Chapter 1 13
  God's Perfect Timing

Chapter 2 67
  The Joy of Family and Friends

Chapter 3 111
  Listening to God's Voice

Chapter 4 157
  Opening Hearts, Building Lives

Chapter 5 197
  God's Goodness in Times of Sadness

Contributors 233

Acknowledgments 235

For the Glory of God
Louis Lotz

IT WAS NOVEMBER—potbellied stove weather, bleak and raw. I was far back in my woods, pruning trees, chopping brambles, tossing brush onto the burn pile, and pulling out the thorns that kept working their way through my cotton gloves and into my palms. The previous week I'd seen leather gloves in the hardware store. But did I purchase a pair? No. Heavy leather gloves—you don't need them until you need them, and then you really need them. It was late afternoon, the gloaming hour. The wind was rising and leafless branches were clawing at the sky. There was a skim of mud on the ground, and my boots were caked and heavy. My feet were cold. It was quitting time.

Gathering up my tools I turned around and began the long walk back to the house for dinner. I had taken only a few steps when I stopped, stunned by the sight. The western sky was aglow with an apricot light, illuminated by a sun already halfway to China. Rows of low, fleecy clouds were bathed in a dazzling, rosy-orange radiance. Monet, on his best day, could not have painted the scene. It was an achingly beautiful sunset. I felt, if only for a moment, like I had touched the hem of heaven. I had been facing one way all afternoon, focusing on wild raspberry canes, scrub trees, brambles, and thorns. But when I turned around and faced the other way—oh my. It was glorious.

Now here is a curious thing. The sun sets every night, but most of the time I don't notice it. It is right there in front of me, but somehow I don't see it. The sun is the largest object in our solar system, a mind-bogglingly enormous sphere of flaming gas held together by its own gravity. It is so large that more than a million planet earths could fit inside it, with room left over for a few thousand Jupiters. Every 24 hours it dips down into the waters of Lake Michigan, or so it seems from my vantage point. How could one possibly not notice this? And yet, again and again, I will observe that darkness has covered the earth, which means the sun has set. And I didn't see it happen.

It strikes me that this incident in the Michigan woods—lifting up my eyes and noticing the sunset—speaks to my spiritual life. God is always there. God is omnipresent—always and everywhere present. As Pascal said of the Almighty, "His center is everywhere; His circumference is nowhere." There is nowhere where God isn't. "Where can I go from your spirit?" says the psalmist. "Where can I free from your presence?" (139:7, NIV). In 1961 the Russian cosmonaut Yuri Gagarin irreverently joked that he didn't see God from the window of his spaceship. "I looked and looked but I did not see God," said Gagarin. I was a teenager at the time, and I remember thinking, *Unzip your spacesuit and you'll see God soon enough.*

God is present in all places at one and the same time, including my life. I have only to lift up my eyes and look. But I am usually facing the wrong way, so to speak, occupied with other things, struggling to deal with the thorns and tangled brush of my life—my doubts and insecurities, grievances and grudges, anger and angst.

I have developed the habit, lately, of reading backward in my journal. That is, in addition to my daily journal writing,

I spend time flipping the pages backward and reading about what was happening in my life months and years ago. And I am surprised at the number of times I have observed, in retrospect, what I failed to see at the time—that God's goodness and grace in my life loomed as large as a billboard, yet somehow I hadn't noticed.

For example, let's take my February 9, 2021, journal entry, where I wrote, with obvious satisfaction and a little surprise, that finally, at long last, I had found myself able to forgive a person who had wronged me. I had limped along for months with inner wounds that refused to heal because I insisted on clinging to my hurt feelings. It's like every morning I picked at the scab, ripped it off, reopened the wound, and felt the hurt all over again, basking self-righteously in the pain. But finally I tired of doing that. I let the wound heal. Truly, I no longer bore any resentment. I wrote that I had forgiven, turned the page, moved on.

Now, that is all well and good, but there was not a word in my journal about how it is God who enables the offended to forgive. A reference to Ephesians 4:32 (NKJV) would have been nice: "And be kind to one another, tenderhearted, forgiving one another, as God in Christ forgave you." It is in God's forgiveness of us that we find the strength to forgive others. But there was no mention of that. The sun had set on my bitterness and hurt, so to speak, but I didn't notice the God who enabled it to happen.

And then there is the April 4, 2020, entry—two-and-a-half pages long!—where I recount the story of how I'd been frustrated because I'd missed out on a certain opportunity, only now to discover that this opportunity had turned sour and was ruinous to the people who were involved. No mention of God's providence, God's protection. No prayer of gratitude for my deliverance. And no repentance for the smug schadenfreude I felt while recounting someone else's misfortune. A minister friend of mine has on his office wall a plaque that reads: *I thank God for protecting me from what I thought I wanted and blessing me with what I didn't know I needed.* I should get myself one of those.

Another example: June 2, 2018, when I wrote about how I lay in bed, in the moonlight, watching my wife sleep, her breathing soft and slow, and how I felt overwhelmed with love for her, and wondered yet again what I had ever done to deserve such a wonderful companion to travel with me on my journey through life. No gratitude to God. No thankfulness for the providence by which I was in the right place at the right time to meet the right person.

And then there was that day in church just last week. A young mother seated in the pew in front of me was holding her baby against her chest, swaying gently, imperceptibly, side to side. The infant was asleep, his head on his mom's shoulder, his face nuzzled in her neck. Suddenly he opened his eyes. He yawned, blinked, stared at me for a long moment, and then gave me a big smile and blew a little bubble. God was present in that child, that smile, that bubble, but I neglected to mention it when I wrote about the incident later that day.

"The whole world is a series of miracles," said Hans Christian Andersen, "but we're so used to them that we call them ordinary things." The sound of my grandson's giggling, the taste of raw honey, the sight of monarch butterflies in the milkweed—how easily miracles become ordinary things. God's goodness and grace are everywhere in my life, pulsing like a quasar, shouting for my attention. *You think I'd notice it more often. Pay attention to how God is present,* I say to myself as I thumb backward through the pages of my journal.

And God is not just present, but active—healing, helping, heartening, surprising me with joy, taking the worst and transforming it for good. "We know that all things work together for good to those who love God," says the apostle Paul (Romans 8:28, NKJV). God is working for my good, for your good. If it's not good, God's not done working. Things may not seem good just now, but one day, perhaps on this side of eternity, perhaps on the other, when God's plan fully unfolds, we will see what our heavenly Father was up to.

I'm making it sound like developing an awareness of God's presence in your life is an easy thing to do. It's not. Some years ago I was invited to meet with a class of senior seminarians to talk with them about the practical aspects of being a pastor. Senior Practicum, the class was called. They had a lot of questions, most of which were pretty predictable. How do you balance your professional life with your family life? What do you say to someone on their deathbed? Where do you get your sermon ideas? Have you ever dropped the communion plate? How do you know when you are *called* by God? (My answer: I cannot define what *calling* is, but I know it when I feel it.)

One question caught me off guard: What is the hardest part of a pastor's job? I'd never thought about that, and I had no prepared answer, but I heard myself say, "The hardest part of the job is getting people to believe that God is at work in their lives."

So many people in the pews will intellectually assent to the Christian faith, but they live like deists. That is, they believe in God, truly they do, but they balk at the idea that God actually enters into their lives, doing the unexpected, the miraculous. Or they will acknowledge that God is able to act in the lives of His children, but they do not really believe that God is able to intervene in *their* lives. Ask people if they believe that God can heal a sick body, and they say yes. Ask if God can save a sick marriage, and they say yes. Ask if God can rebuild a ruined relationship between parent and child, brother and sister. Yes, they believe that. But they struggle to believe that such divine intervention can take place in *their own lives.* Scripture is replete with stories of how God intervenes in human affairs—helping, healing, transforming, saving. But our own lives are so familiar, so common, and it is difficult to sense the mystery of God pulsing through them. But friend, God *does* intervene. Invite Him to intervene in your situation. God is active all the time, everywhere, including your life.

There are days when I don't notice the sunset. But that doesn't mean the sun did not set. It means I wasn't paying attention. I was facing the wrong way, pulling at thorns, struggling with the brambles that pluck at my sleeve. And when I find myself thinking that the omnipresent God is not present and active in my life, then one of two things must be true: either my life is the one place in all creation where God is absent, or I am not paying attention. I figure it's the latter. That's why I am trying to be more attentive, expectantly and prayerfully looking for God every day.

This book that you hold in your hands helps me in that endeavor. Here are authors who have experienced everyday miracles of healing and helping, encouragement and transformation. Here are men and women just like you who have felt the brush of angel's wings, and who have looked around in their lives and said, with Jacob, "Surely the LORD is in this place and I did not know it" (Genesis 28:16, NKJV). Here are authors who have experienced sorrow and pain, but who came to see how God was at work in their sadness, taking the worst and using it for some redemptive purpose, and who can say, with Joseph, "Even though you intended to do harm to me, God intended it for good" (Genesis 50:20, NRSVUE). I am grateful to these authors, and to the Guideposts organization, for helping me to find and celebrate God's presence in my life.

On a bookshelf in my office I have a small volume given to me when I was a child: the 1937 devotional classic *A Diary of Private Prayer* by the Scottish theologian John Baillie. It was a gift from my paternal grandmother, a woman passionately committed to her little grandson's spiritual well-being. Grandma seemed to think that my parents were not sufficiently invested in my religious upbringing, and she strove relentlessly to correct this deficiency. She was always giving me gifts like Bible story coloring books, ceramic angel figurines that clamped to the headboard of your bed and looked down on you as you slept, phonograph records of George Beverly Shea singing great hymns of the faith ("Abide With Me," "How Great Thou Art," and the like), and prayer books like *A Diary of Private Prayer*. Grandma even went so far as to pay me money for memorizing Bible verses, a practice that gave new meaning to the phrase "the value of Scripture." One penny per verse was the going rate, as I recall. A lot of money in those days.

A Diary of Private Prayer offers prayers for every day of the month: 31 morning prayers, 31 evening prayers. It is an old book, and the language is old-fashioned. Paging through the book, I came upon these words in the Morning Prayer for Day 16: "Give me, O God, this day a strong and vivid sense that Thou art by my side. In multitude and in solitude, in business and in leisure, in my downsitting and in my upstanding, may I ever be aware of Thine accompanying presence." I don't recall if those words spoke to me when I was a child, but they do now. God is by my side. God is everywhere, in everything. There is nowhere He is not. When challenges come we can rest secure in this: The Lord is right there, active, involved, healing and helping, taking the worst and using it for good.

I'm pretty sure I walked home with a smile on that November day, enjoying the sunset that God had so graciously provided, embraced by His light, to use the title of this book. A final few leaves had come unattached in the wind, and floated lazily down like goldfish swimming in a bowl. Toadstools jutting up from an old decaying log resembled tiny tables and chairs, like furniture for a dollhouse, and raccoon tracks in the mud looked like little hands.

Walking along, savoring the sunset, I announced to myself that "The heavens are telling the glory of God, and the firmament proclaims his handiwork" (Psalm 19:1, NRSVUE). I vowed to be more attentive to those moments when the glory of God was staring me in the face. I began mentally composing the journal entry that I would write after dinner, about being more alert to the ways God's grace and glory pervade my life. And somewhere along the way I realized that my feet didn't feel quite so cold anymore.

We pray. We wait. We hope.
We believe. And in His perfect
time, we see His faithful
plan unfold.

—Anitha Abraham

CHAPTER 1
God's Perfect Timing

Dual Blessings. 14
    Bettie Boswell

Blessed Be the Name of the Lord 18
    Joyce Farinella

My Blue Shoes. 24
    Brenda Glanzer Lilliston, as told to
    Angela J. Kaufman

Out of the Darkness 29
    Poppy Webb

Time to Write 36
    Cynthia A. Lovely

Adventures with God 41
    Elizabeth Erlandson

God's Faithfulness to Lead Us 48
    Lisa Lenning

God's Guiding Hand to a Home 54
    Laurie Herlich

The Gift of a Slow Elevator. 60
    Sandy Kirby Quandt

Dual Blessings
Bettie Boswell

When I first graduated college with a church music degree, I never dreamed I'd end up as a teacher, but that's what I did. After a few years at home raising my babies, I went back to college to acquire my teacher's degree. I decided to prepare to be an elementary teacher, since I enjoyed working with that age group at church. During the course of taking classes, I added enough credits to receive a certificate in teaching music. As it turned out, both licensures would be just what God had planned for my new career.

My first few years after graduating with a master's degree, I taught young students in classrooms. Student teaching led to a position as a teacher's aide, and soon I had an offer for a full-time position teaching music for a public school. It was a traveling teacher assignment, which increased my car driving confidence. That ability would prove important later in life. I also grew as a teacher, developing music lessons that would serve me well for the rest of my career.

A few years later, my husband's career took us to another state. I worried about how difficult it would be to find a music teaching position, especially since I wanted to teach only young children. My fears proved justified. However, God provided. My husband's income had increased and, thanks to the fact that I'd maintained a certification for elementary education, I obtained a position teaching first grade in a Christian school.

The experience was a positive one. The Christian school teachers needed to provide music for their own classrooms. When they discovered I taught music, several arranged to do some exchange teaching. My first graders experienced Spanish lessons and fun literature activities while I taught a fifth- and third-grade class about music.

When my husband's job required us to relocate and I found myself job hunting again, having both licenses gave me a big advantage. During the summer we moved, I spent much of the time interviewing and sending resumes. Days before school started, I had a final interview. The principal loved the fact that I had the two licenses because the school had an emphasis on cooperative learning between subject areas. Within an hour after the interview, she called. The job was mine.

> "For I know the plans I have for you," declares the LORD, "plans to prosper you and not to harm you, plans to give you hope and a future."
>
> —JEREMIAH 29:11 (NIV)

Having the background of teaching in the classroom helped me create music that both fit my music curriculum and supported classroom knowledge. The art teacher and I worked with the fourth-grade team to create exciting history-based programs complete with field trips, accompanied by music and art programs. My students and I enjoyed the learning experiences. I had a supportive principal who valued my contributions to the school. I hoped this would be where I could spend all of my final years before retiring.

At that point it had been many years since I used my elementary teaching license, and I thought about letting that certification drop. But something—or Someone—told me I needed to renew that option.

Then Covid-19 struck. Teachers and students abandoned the buildings and headed home. I created video lessons and became adept at online instruction during the remainder of the spring semester. The students joined a virtual classroom and responded to my lessons. But by August, the virus still raged, and schools had to make hard decisions.

> Each of you should use whatever gift you have received to serve others, as faithful stewards of God's grace in its various forms.
>
> —1 PETER 4:10 (NIV)

I was driving home from an inspiring retreat when my dashboard started pinging with text notices from my fellow music teachers. Out of the corner of my eye I saw words like *cut* and *part-time*. Then my phone rang. My heart raced as I pulled into a nearby rest stop. My principal was on the phone with news of cuts to my music position.

I trembled as I listened to his apologetic explanation. My racing mind reminded me that this was my last year before retiring. My income from the coming year would play a big factor in my retirement pension.

That's when I understood why I'd been prompted to renew my elementary license. I had options. I breathed a prayer of thanks to God. Then I interrupted my principal's spiel to say that I wanted to take an open classroom position in the district. He was surprised.

In fact, I surprised many people. A longtime music teacher taking on a second-grade classroom position seemed inconceivable. Later I would find out administrators had worried that it would lead to disaster. But I had the licensure and the experience, and I was in first position on the seniority list when it came to elementary teaching.

Being over 60 allowed me the opportunity to teach students online from my house. This also provided extra protection for me from the virus. Using my long-ago experience as a primary teacher, I headed to a vacant classroom and gathered needed texts and supplies. Using the knowledge of teaching online I'd gained during the previous quarter, I prepared virtual lessons, worksheets, and activities. I jumped in and started teaching my students.

Two weeks into the semester I received an email from the administration. Parents were impressed. The district had hired two new teachers for the other virtual second-grade classes, and they needed help. Would I be a mentor for the rest of the year? I agreed. Blessing others is part of the Christian walk.

> **You make known to me the path of life; you will fill me with joy in your presence, with eternal pleasures at your right hand.**
>
> —PSALM 16:11 (NIV)

A godly reminder to renew both licenses every 5 years had blessed me. Those choices led to a career that fulfilled me and provided a nice retirement.

Be a blessing to those around you. Know that God has your best interests in mind as you travel through life. You never know when something from the past will prove beneficial in the present.

Blessed Be the Name of the Lord

Joyce Farinella

"Yes!" My voice trembled as I spoke to my caseworker about the placement of a 2-week-old baby girl. This was the phone call I had prayed for. I had no idea that my biggest challenges and most important lesson were still yet to come.

I had always wanted to adopt a child. My father had been orphaned at a young age, which made a big impression on me even in my childhood. I assumed I would get married, have biological children with my husband, and then adopt. As I reached adulthood, I always seemed to be trying to catch up with where I thought I should be. I didn't start college until I was 24, graduating 4 years later with a BS in Business Administration. I was 30 when I moved to a larger city, where I figured I would find Mr. Right.

That didn't happen though. Only the wrong kind of men noticed me, while those I thought could be a good match chose other women. I struggled with loneliness as I watched friends get married and have children. It felt like God had abandoned me. Finally, in desperation, I cried out to Him: "God, if You don't want me to get married, take this desire away. I'm tired of being miserable."

In time, He answered that plea, and I was able to accept my life as a single woman. I overcame the desire to get married, yet I still had one regret—that I would never have children. Little did I know that things were about to change in a way I didn't expect.

A friend mentioned that she knew someone who was pregnant who didn't want to keep the baby. After I adjusted to the idea of being a single mother, I let her know I was interested in adopting. Though cautious at first, I grew excited by the prospect of being a mother. Then came the fateful day when the woman changed her mind and kept the baby. Though disheartened, the situation was the match that lit a fire in my life to consider the possibility of adoption.

> **Give thanks in all circumstances; for this is God's will for you in Christ Jesus.**
>
> —1 THESSALONIANS 5:18 (NIV)

I decided to learn how I could adopt even though I wasn't married. Private adoptions were expensive, and I learned it would be highly unlikely that the birth mother would consider an unmarried woman. Fostering to adopt had minimal cost and was open to single people. One day, my sister came to me.

"I heard on the radio that there's an informational meeting about fostering to adopt," she said.

I made plans to attend. On a warm day in June, I drove an hour away and sat in on a meeting that explained the basics of the foster-to-adopt program. The speakers told stories of children of all ages who were adopted through foster care. Intrigued, I wanted to learn more.

Back at home, I found out that I would need to attend classes to get my foster care license. The agency at the informational meeting was based in St. Louis, 2 hours from where I lived. I would have to make long trips to attend the required 10-week classes. Even that didn't discourage me, though I knew it would be quite an undertaking.

As I prayed about whether it was God's will for me to commit to this process, the agency contacted me and let me know they had workers in my county to conduct the training. What an answer to prayer! I felt that God was letting me know that He was with me on this path as I signed up for the next available training session.

> **And the LORD, He is the One who goes before you. He will be with you. He will not leave you nor forsake you; do not fear nor be dismayed.**
>
> —DEUTERONOMY 31:8 (NKJV)

The intense training, held one night a week, lasted between 3 and 4 hours, with homework to be completed for the next session. The trainers discussed the challenges of children in foster care, helping potential foster parents to be prepared for what they would be facing, stressing that most babies went to two-parent foster homes. Though my heart longed for a baby, I resolved to take in any child who needed a home. My license would be for females from birth to age 17, increasing my chance for a placement. I began praying for the child who God meant for me. I never asked for a baby, instead focusing on receiving a healthy child.

After I completed the training, the home study, and other requirements to receive my license, I waited. It didn't take long until I begin receiving placement calls, but none of the opportunities were the right fit. Some were sibling groups too large for the only bedroom I had available for a child. I accepted some teen placements only to have those fail for reasons out of my control. As the months passed, it seemed I would never get a child to fill my home and my heart. Had I misunderstood God's leading? Had He forgotten about me?

> May the LORD cause you to flourish, both you and your children.
>
> —PSALM 115:14 (NIV)

During this time, I began having issues with my car. The heater stopped working in the dead of winter. Then the transmission started to fail. It seemed my car troubles were another obstacle standing in my way since I couldn't accept a placement if I didn't have safe and reliable transportation. So I focused on finding another car. Once again, God answered my prayer when I found a cute little sports car, a silver Saturn Ion.

As I drove the car home one cold winter morning, I noticed a missed call. I played back the message from my caseworker.

"There's a 2-week-old baby girl who needs to be placed right away. I wanted to see if you were interested."

Tears rolled down my face and my hands were shaking as I called her back. "Yes!" I nearly shouted into the phone. God hadn't forgotten me.

The caseworker arrived at 2:30 that afternoon and handed me a tiny baby girl with a head of dark brown hair. I fell in love immediately even as I heard the caseworker talking about scheduling visits with the biological mother.

I knew the goal of foster care was reunification between child and biological parent. But I couldn't stop my heart from falling in love with this tiny person who relied on me for her every need. Over the next few months, I faithfully took her to the scheduled visits. Many times, the mother never showed up. Hope blossomed in my heart, though I felt guilty at the same time.

I got to know this young mother through our visits, and as I saw her struggles I realized she wasn't the enemy. God tugged on my heart as He showed me that He loved her too. I began to pray for this mother to turn her life around even as my heart ached, knowing that I would lose this precious baby if she succeeded.

During this time, I held onto Job 1:21 (ESV), which says, "The Lord gave and the Lord has taken away; blessed be the name of the Lord." I knew I was supposed to praise God amid uncertainty and believe in His goodness even if things didn't turn out the way I wanted. As my emotions went up and down like a roller coaster, I felt His presence and stayed calm as I waited to learn what would happen next.

After months of raising this little girl and not knowing of our future together, the caseworker told me they were going to recommend adoption instead of reunification. The mother knew she wasn't in the best place to be a parent, and she gave up her parental rights. I was overjoyed and praised God for answering the longing of my heart while teaching me to trust in Him throughout the process.

GOD'S GIFT OF SIGHT
— Kimberly Shumate —

WHEN ABRAHAM AND his family came into the Promised Land after a generation had passed in the wilderness, they were given all they surveyed. Everything, as far as their eyes could see, was now theirs—promised not only to them, but also to their descendants, who God told Abraham would be as numerous as the grains of dust on the ground (Genesis 13:16). When we have the faith to believe it—when we go where we are led by the Lord, giving thanks and praise along the way, as Abraham did—God can and will give us the blessings that we visualize in our mind's eye.

Two days before the little girl's first birthday, we stood in the courtroom where the judge spoke the words that changed my life: "This child shall be given all the same rights and privileges as if she were born to you." God blessed me with the most perfect gift, a daughter who I will love always and the knowledge that He will be beside me every step of the way.

My Blue Shoes

Brenda Glanzer Lilliston, as told to Angela J. Kaufman

Today is a normal day if you consider attending a funeral service routine. As a former pastor and now a hospital chaplain, I am accustomed to these phases of life. On this morning, the celebration of life is being held at a nursing home about 40 miles away. As I drive to the location, my mind is thinking of the few residents I know who live there. One lady in particular, Ida, keeps popping up in my thoughts.

I don't have time to visit her, God. I have a long day ahead of me.

My conversations with God have become more common as I struggle with health issues. There is a fine line between what I want to accomplish each day and how much fatigue my body can endure.

Maybe if there is time after the service, I can stop by and see her.

I have been privileged to hear the stories of God's mystery and miracles from people I have served for almost 2 decades. Being a minister places me in the unusual space of meeting others in vulnerable times. The joy and honor of being considered a safe person for others to share these intimate faith accounts with is one of the highlights of being in ministry.

Today, though, time is not on my side. The service runs long, and I am allowed a limited time off from the hospital. However, I continue to feel this nudge of insistence that I need to see Ida.

Okay, God. I'll find her room.

Leaving the nursing home chapel, I wander through a few hallways to her residential wing. My sense of urgency is increased when I find out she is not in her room. A quick backtrack to the nearest nurses' station provides the direction I need. She is eating lunch in a small cafeteria down the hall.

Maybe she won't be there either.

As I walk in, she looks up, recognizes who I am, and immediately says, "I dreamed about my blues shoes last night." I swallow my surprise at this unusual greeting and respond with a cheery "Hello, Ida."

Ida made an impression on me as a member of the church I had pastored. She had taken me aside and encouraged me in my gifts as a woman in ministry. She had a deep faith and shared life stories that resulted from dreams she knew God had given her. We both sensed God's guidance through dreams, and it was a source of strong spiritual connection for us.

Ida's life was full of prayer and meditation, and her extroverted personality empowered her to share her faith with others. Her spiritual gift of encouraging people to keep their eyes on Jesus, especially through difficult times, was based

> **Finally, brothers and sisters, whatever is true, whatever is noble, whatever is right, whatever is pure, whatever is lovely, whatever is admirable—if anything is excellent or praiseworthy—think about such things.**
>
> —PHILIPPIANS 4:8 (NIV)

on the verse from Lamentations 3:22–23 (NIV): "Because of the Lord's great love we are not consumed, for his compassions never fail. They are new every morning; great is your faithfulness."

When I switched from pastoring to chaplaincy a number of years ago, this new ministry of service felt as comfortable as a pair of well-worn shoes. A few months after starting to work at a brand-new hospital, I found Ida's name listed on the hospital census. Our bond grew as we reconnected and she shared with me one of her life verses: "But this I call to mind, and therefore I have hope" (Lamentations 3:21, RSV). Joy was evident in her life, and people loved to be around her warmth and fun outlook.

What a treasure she is, God, I think as my mind returns to the present moment.

Ida persists in the direction of our conversation. I have not known her to struggle with memory issues. However, she is in her 80s. Perhaps I caught her at a bad time.

She tells me she is missing her favorite, most comfortable blue shoes, last seen during her hospital stay. I was a familiar face during that time of her life, and therefore, I understand the connection she makes with me and her shoes.

After a difficult monthlong stay in the hospital, and another month in her current facility, she began to have the clarity of mind to ask her children to go look for her shoes. They showed

> **Indeed, the very hairs of your head are all numbered. Don't be afraid; you are worth more than many sparrows.**
>
> —LUKE 12:7 (NIV)

concern and understanding, but felt it was unlikely the hospital would have kept her personal items through this length of time.

Now here I am, 1 year later, standing in front of her, the exact day after her vivid dream about the blue shoes. My mind races with questions. *Where could they be? Who would you ask? A security guard? A housekeeping supervisor?* I know a positive outcome is not likely.

I sense her loss and realize the long stay in this nursing home has only exacerbated the lack of joy that something familiar and comforting can provide. Ida has always had a special place in my heart, and so I agree to try to find them for her.

I am eager to return to work at the hospital to investigate the lost shoes even though I know finding them is a long shot.

> **I wait for the LORD, my whole being waits, and in his word I put my hope.**
>
> —PSALM 130:5 (NIV)

God, I know you have always provided for Ida throughout her life. I trust You are in the details of her request.

As I turn to walk down a corridor, I find myself meeting a security guard I recognize. Once I explain my predicament, he acknowledges a lack of procedures for lost items, but offers to bring me to a place he knows where they are taken. He leads me to the back of the hospital, to a loading dock where there are two lockers. As he opens each door, we see numerous bags with people's names still taped on them. We proceed to go through every single one, but it is not until we are at the bottom of the pile, looking at the very last bag, that we see Ida's name and find her blue shoes inside. My breath catches as I feel God's presence.

Your timing is incredible, God. You never consider any desire too small.

The next weekend, I return to Ida's nursing home. God moving in mysterious ways may seem like a coincidence to some, but I am not concerned about that type of reaction from Ida. As I walk into her room with a sack under my arms, she asks, "Did you find my blue shoes?"

She is so happy, utterly thrilled, you would have thought I brought her a bag full of money. The simple joy and comfort of these returned shoes becomes a story of faith she shares with those who visit her. Six months later, I run into another former parishioner, who relates how Ida told them all about our adventures with God as we found her shoes.

How grateful I am to have followed divine leading, even though I was pressed for time. At every turn, God provided the best timing, the correct people, and the physical strength to be an intricate part of Ida's answer to prayer.

As the years have passed and Ida has joined her loving God, I remember her blue shoes and the promise of hope and a future God has given each of us.

Out of the Darkness
Poppy Webb

The suicide plan was set. It would be clean and away from home. My workplace offered the best location. An ultra-low-temperature freezer down the hall from my lab was the "weapon" of choice. I read that dying from hypothermia feels like going to sleep, so maybe I could just close my eyes and drift away. My body wouldn't be discovered until one of my colleagues opened the freezer to store a batch of cell cultures.

I smirked, envisioning the horror on Dr. Ahmed's face when he looked at my lifeless body. I also imagined the tearful faces of my loved ones, especially my husband and mother. Guilt and sadness engulfed me at that thought. They didn't deserve my selfish resolution, but they also didn't deserve my unexplained moodiness. Over the past few months, I'd sunk into a dangerous place of vengeful resentment, with bitterness at the core of my self-righteous attitude. I knew how to do my job and how to do it well, but with the change in personnel, I felt my primary responsibilities had been diverted. The patient always came first along with my loyalty to the institution. Now, both felt challenged. A sense of hopelessness and despair burrowed its way into my being.

It all started when Dr. Ahmed was named the director of the specialty laboratory within the academic medical center where I worked. He was a logical choice since the previous director had been serving in an interim capacity. Dr. Ahmed's medical expertise and research prowess were commendable and well-known in the medical center. However, his bullying tactics and arrogance could be considered irritating to some.

With his appointment, Dr. Ahmed became the director of a hospital lab as well as a research lab (in addition to being my boss), so he and I crossed paths in our work. I questioned his work ethic, wondering why he allowed his research to bleed over into clinical testing, thus impacting me. I knew it wasn't right for him to take advantage of dedicated hospital funds to further his research interests. Anger and judgment stirred within me whenever he walked into the room. His attitude annoyed me, but his faith annoyed me more. He was an active leader in his non-Christian church. Truthfully, his faith should not have annoyed me but it did. I was probably just looking for something to fault him for.

I viewed his actions as crossing over an imaginary line separating good and evil, and I wanted no part of what I felt was an abuse of his power, my time, and the medical center's money. Nonetheless, I was obligated to comply with his requests or risk being dismissed for insubordination.

While this struggle within me may sound trivial, it was very real and affected me in ways I have a hard time expressing. I considered being a whistleblower, but figured no one would listen. I was only a lab tech, and he was a medical provider and a researcher with grant money. I thought I'd be laughed right out of a job.

Believing I had no outlet for expression, I fell deeper and deeper into a pit of despair, depression, and guilt. It was as if I had two different personalities. Guilt clawed at my ungodly and perverted viewpoints. I knew God could not approve of my thoughts and behavior, but I couldn't help how I felt. I'd inadvertently let someone creep in to take God's place by controlling my mind and actions.

I was conflicted. Sure, I could transfer to another department, but that was not the answer. Any job change I made should be on my terms—be my choice—not a reaction, especially to someone for whom I had no respect. My long-term goals to advance in my workplace would not be thwarted. I refused to yield to the power I allowed Dr. Ahmed to have over me. My struggle intensified knowing that God should be the only one who has that power.

How did I get to this point where God, the giver of life, the creator of all, was not the One who filled my mind with thoughts of peace, love, and hope? I despised how my life was now controlled by someone other than God. I couldn't tolerate it any longer. There seemed to me to be only one way to resolve this paradox—suicide.

> **You have rescued me from death; you have kept my feet from slipping. So now I can walk in your presence, O God, in your life-giving light.**
>
> —PSALM 56:13 (NLT)

Although I wore my "mask" well, those closest to me, including my husband, could tell something was wrong. The only person I could discuss my issues with was my best friend Sandra, who was also my supervisor. (That was because she knew Dr. Ahmed well. She worked as his lab tech in his research lab before becoming the supervisor in the specialty lab where I worked.) After much coercion, Sandra convinced me to speak to her Christian friend. Tired of the months of badgering, I agreed.

Sandra set up the meeting. Still reluctant, I met with Sandra's friend in her home. I don't recall her name or much of the conversation, but the truth of her friend's words lingered in my mind. She told me she was glad I had no self-esteem left so that God could fill the void.

"You need God-esteem," she said.

What?

The words "You need God-esteem" annoyed me at first. They even aroused some anger. How could this woman who didn't know me have the audacity to say such things? I mean, I loved God. I loved Him more than myself. At least I thought I did. But did I love Him more than my pride? Questions swirled in my mind. Was she right?

After allowing her words to settle in my mind over the next few days and pushing through my annoyance, I began to adopt her words as a mantra. The phrase popped in and out of my head more and more as the days went by. I felt an urgency welling up inside to correct this flaw that had been uncovered. In an effort to develop God-esteem, it would require God's Word, a source of light and hope. It was time to open my Bible again and pray.

Having tried before without success, I determined this time to try harder. I slotted a specific time to read the Bible each morning before going to work. I had not done this before. My commitment level was no longer shaky and sporadic; it was solid this time. Whatever it took, however long it took, I was going to see God's work in my heart. And I vowed to make my prayers faith-filled this time, not just empty words.

Flipping through the pages of my Bible, I sat in the bedroom chair reading a psalm or two—short ones, of course.

Anything too long was intolerable. I knew the Psalms were easy to read and understand and thought they would help me focus on praise to God. Praying was hard too—the words wouldn't come. Perhaps if I got on my knees, it would help. So I tried that but still the words remained stuck in my throat. "Help" was all I could mutter.

Keeping things short and sweet at the beginning meant a more successful outcome. I was slow in my progression, but I was compelled to believe it was in God's time. He knew I needed to take it slow in order for my wounds to heal and the darkness to dispel.

Though my efforts were feeble, I committed daily to search the Bible and attempted to pray. Progress seemed elusive and slow at the beginning, and I was compelled to believe this was the timing God intended. His presence continued to gnaw at me and I felt Him honor my persistence. After glancing at verses in the Old and New Testaments without much interest, I happened upon a verse in First Peter: "Therefore, prepare your minds for action, keep sober in spirit, set your hope completely on the grace to be brought to you at the revelation of Jesus Christ" (1 Peter 1:13, NASB). I could not ignore the phrase "set your hope completely." Nor could I

> **I pray that the eyes of your heart may be enlightened, so that you will know what is the hope of His calling, what are the riches of the glory of His inheritance in the saints.**
>
> —EPHESIANS 1:18 (NASB)

ignore the fact that I was not "sober in spirit." My spirit was clouded, lacking clarity.

As weeks progressed, my prayers did too. They evolved from one word into a sentence, then a few more sentences, until I was reaching a point of discussion with God. He impressed upon me that I should pray for my "enemy." Ouch! I wanted no good to come to Dr. Ahmed. *He doesn't deserve my prayers, God; he doesn't even know or love You.* I forced myself to pray for him anyway, with the satisfaction of knowing vengeance belongs to the Lord.

God took His time to accommodate my stepwise healing. And I came to realize that His time frame for my healing coincided with my need to develop God-esteem as I learned what it meant to live my life glorifying Him. Bitterness began to melt so I could at least acknowledge Dr. Ahmed's presence when I passed him on the sidewalk or in the hall. The delineation between research and clinical work became less of a factor. I learned to accept the impact of a large medical center within the political arena. And my self-righteous attitude softened. Recognizing my invisible signs of depression, I handed them over to God one by one.

> **Heal me, LORD, and I will be healed; save me, and I will be saved, for you are the one I praise.**
>
> —JEREMIAH 17:14 (NIV)

Over time, the mask disappeared, my thoughts were less condemning, and my conversations became genuine. Whether noticeable or not, interaction and communication within my relationships improved. I was being transformed. My mind, heart, and soul were becoming reunited.

My depression took almost 2 years to go away, the length of time I've heard it takes without medication, something I chose not to do. My medication became my meditation in God's Word. I leaned on 1 Peter 1:13 daily until grace was brought to me "at the revelation of Jesus Christ." God brought me back into real living and back into my real self.

My family and friends never knew the depth of my darkness those many years ago. I never shared my plans of suicide with anyone until now. I write these words under a different name because I still don't want them to know. I also used different names for the individuals mentioned in my story. I share this story because I understand firsthand that Christians are not immune to dark places. Courage and persistence are required to step out of the darkness into God's guiding light. If we are willing to look, we will find that the glimmer becomes a gleaming light that leads toward restoration and forgiveness.

With God now guiding my life, I don't allow myself to compromise my witness, my family, or my life. And He is using me today to glorify His name through international mission work, writing, music, singing, and teaching.

When I retired from the medical center several years ago, guess who spoke at my retirement reception? Yep, Dr. Ahmed. We are friends today, both professionally and personally. Dr. Ahmed knows something happened but doesn't exactly know what or how. God changed me, lifting me out of the darkness to live again in His glorious light.

Time to Write
Cynthia A. Lovely

"Yay, I won!"

I jumped up from my desk chair, paced in circles around my office, and did a jig. Fortunately, there were not a lot of people at work that early in the morning to see the display of enthusiasm. I read the email again while alternating between laughter and tears.

"Congratulations, you are one of the winners of the Cecil Murphey scholarships to the Blue Ridge Mountains Christian Writer's Conference." The email stated that my essay had been chosen and listed the details of the scholarship with a request for a response for acceptance. My fingers flew over the keys as I returned an immediate and grateful reply.

I grabbed the phone and called my husband but punched in the wrong number. I tried again and when he answered, I was talking so fast I wasn't making much sense. He finally convinced me to slow down so he could understand my exciting news. We rejoiced together. This scholarship not only made the conference a sure thing but also increased my belief that God wanted me to attend. Perhaps my dream of writing was truly a possibility. Now definite plans could be set in motion.

Travel arrangements were made and the date finally arrived. The flight was only a few hours and we set up with our car rental with no problem. Driving through the Blue Ridge

Mountains was lovely, and my expectations for the conference rose higher along with the mountains surrounding us. As soon as I stepped on the grounds of the retreat center I could feel the rush of excitement.

That week I felt like I was in a different world, a different country even! I was immersed in the wonderful world of writers, and I loved every bit of it. It was informative, inspiring, and exhausting—and way beyond my comfort zone. Yet I pressed onward, knowing God had planned it all out for me. And it truly helped to have my supportive husband with me whenever I started to have an insecurity meltdown.

One of my major reasons for attending this conference was to establish a Christian foundation in my writing. I was continually reminded that week that our writing was for the Lord, not for ourselves. The focus was completely in line with my heart's desire. The staff was excellent, the speakers were motivational, and the editors and publishers were kind and helpful. It was a blessing to mingle with other new writers and share dreams and aspirations.

> **The unfolding of your words gives light, it gives understanding to the simple.**
>
> —PSALM 119:130 (NIV)

I remember taking a break midweek when I came upon a sheltered nook with a wooden swing tucked away from the crowds. I was unable to resist the lure of the peaceful setting and nestled into the swing with a sigh of relief. The gentle swaying motion of the swing calmed my heart and my jumbled thoughts from the overload of lessons. Distant murmurs of conversation from students returning to class faded away until all was quiet.

I tilted my head back to look up at the blue sky and caught the faint fragrance of the flowers lining the pathway. The sun felt warm upon my face as a cool breeze murmured through the tree branches.

Ah . . . peace. Words of encouragement from recent speakers flitted across my mind as I swayed back and forth. One teacher had emphasized, "If you write, you are a writer." I shuffled my feet to slow the swing while clinging to the rough wood. "I am a writer." It sounded good out loud. No one argued the statement and the birds chirped their agreement in pleasant tones.

Smiling to myself, I kicked back into motion, repeating the sentence and allowing it to sink into my heart.

> **Trust in the LORD with all thine heart; and lean not unto thine own understanding. In all thy ways acknowledge him, and he shall direct thy paths.**
>
> —PROVERBS 3:5–6 (KJV)

I recalled all the inspiring messages telling me this was true. The wonderful surprise of winning a scholarship to the conference. *I am a writer.* My encouraging friends and cowriters. *I am a writer.* The joy of my first published article. *I am a writer.* The memories formed a marching beat to the rhythm of the swing.

Suddenly I stopped as the culmination of events and experiences came clearly into focus. There was no longer a question or a stumbling over the phrase. Years of doubts and insecurities had been slipping off my shoulders to bring me to this place of truth. A definite shifting occurred inside me, like a puzzle

GOD'S GIFT OF HEARING
— Lynne Hartke —

A PERSON CAN calculate the distance to a storm by counting the seconds between a lightning flash and the rumble of thunder. Sound travels approximately 1 mile every 5 seconds. Therefore, the distance in miles can be determined by dividing the tabulated number of seconds by 5. "The voice of the Lord is over the waters; the God of glory thunders, the Lord thunders over the mighty waters," the psalmist wrote in Psalm 29:3 (NIV). How wonderful we have ears to hear God's thunder that enable us to seek safety during a storm.

---

piece fitting perfectly into place. This scene from the conference remains etched in my memory and in my spirit.

After the conference, my husband and I enjoyed several vacation days together. We stayed at the retreat center and had plenty of relaxing time to reflect on the week. I left the center determined to pursue my love of writing and follow the path God had opened up for me.

After traveling a bit and visiting friends we drove to the airport. We had several hours until flight time so we wandered around the airport for a while. Upon entering the food court, I found a table and sat down. My eyes immediately focused on a huge sign hanging in the air: Time to Write.

Stunned, I sat frozen in awe. I don't think I would have been surprised to hear the audible voice of God. He was definitely getting my attention with this heavenly billboard. Coming out

> **Delight thyself also in the LORD: and he shall give thee the desires of thine heart.**
>
> —PSALM 37:4 (KJV)

of my stupor, I glanced around and realized I had sat down right by a display for Cross pens, and this huge sign was above the rack. God surely has a sense of humor.

"Yes, Lord," I said in total agreement. No more excuses. It's time to write.

Adventures with God
Elizabeth Erlandson

Boom! The fire alarm shrieked and seconds later, water gushed from the sprinkler system, drenching boxes of candy, precious inventory from around the world. The roof at Licorice International had caved in.

My business partner, Ardith, and I raced out the front door, just in time to see fire trucks converging on our narrow cobblestone street. The firemen set up barriers and began wrapping the perimeter of our historic three-story brick building with wide yellow tape.

"No one, absolutely no one, is to enter that building until it has been thoroughly inspected," the chief warned. "The building could implode."

We later learned that repairmen had overloaded one area of the roof with excess equipment, causing a portion to collapse. Thankfully, no one had been injured. The building passed inspection and 8 days later, all the tenants returned to their businesses. The water damage to our area was minimal and insurance made up for most of our losses. Once again, God protected Ardith and me from calamity.

Ardith is my best friend, business partner, and prayer partner. We've been praying together since 1991. We met several months after a women's retreat at our church. Ardith hadn't attended, but at the end of the meeting, several women insisted that I had to meet her. "You two have so much in common," they said.

Ardith had shared her testimony at the previous year's retreat, and like me, she had lived a worldly life before committing to Christ. Sin—that's what we had in common. But looking back more than 30 years now, the most obvious thing we had in common was our age; we were half a generation older than the other ladies in our church.

When Ardith and I finally met, I was sure we would never be friends. She seemed sophisticated, had a high-speed job, and traveled extensively. Her husband and children were good-looking and dressed fashionably.

> **Many are the plans in a person's heart, but it is the LORD's purpose that prevails.**
>
> —PROVERBS 19:21 (NIV)

I worked as a writer at Back to the Bible, a Christian ministry. My husband, a former professor and pastor, stayed home with our children. We struggled to get by on my salary and my husband's side gig, selling baseball cards at flea markets. Our kids were cute but we weren't fancy.

My inferiority complex kicked in, and I resisted becoming friends.

Then my father-in-law died and we had to drive from Lincoln, Nebraska, to Chicago, Illinois, for the funeral. The day before we left, Ardith came to our house with a basket of treats for the trip. Her kindness touched me and I told God that even though I didn't expect to make friends in Lincoln (I always wanted to move back East, closer to my family), if He decided to give me one, Ardith would be okay. Little did I know how okay she would be.

Ardith's thoughtful gesture opened the door to our becoming better acquainted, and we began talking on the phone. We rarely saw each other because of our schedules, but our friendship grew through praying together on the phone.

We had been prayer partners for 10 years when we each arrived at a career crossroads. She had worked for an international auction house for more than 20 years and had gained expertise in accounting, human resources, and facilitating complex negotiations. When the business changed hands, she helped with the transition and decided against joining the new company. She wanted a different kind of challenge.

As the public relations writer for a worldwide radio ministry, I had cultivated marketing and fundraising skills. Later, as the development director for a large homeless shelter, I learned how to garner free publicity and win favor in the community. When my boss accepted another job, I decided to become a consultant to not-for-profit organizations. That's when Ardith and I became business partners.

We set aside a day to map out our plan and drove together to a state park midway between Lincoln and Omaha. We felt

> **Therefore do not worry about tomorrow, for tomorrow will worry about itself. Each day has enough trouble of its own.**
>
> —MATTHEW 6:34 (NIV)

confident that God would show us what He had in mind (or, more accurately, confirm what we had already decided).

We had everything we needed, including a strategic planning "arrow" designed to point us in the right direction. We listed our personal and professional achievements, our goals for the next 5 years, and the challenges we might encounter. We also did a rudimentary SWOT analysis (strengths, weaknesses, opportunities, and threats). We were ready! We were on our way to becoming business consultants.

> **I will instruct you and teach you in the way you should go; I will counsel you with my eye upon you.**
>
> —PSALM 32:8 (ESV)

Just as we were ready to wrap up our meeting, we accidentally tipped the table, and coffee spilled all over our awesome arrow. Once the shock of our mini disaster passed and we wiped up the mess, we laughed and recognized that God must have other plans for us. For the next 6 months, we explored our options and asked God to make His will for us clear.

One day in 2001, while ordering candy for my husband for Christmas, I spoke with a man in New York who owned a mail-order licorice business. He wanted to sell his company and I suggested he sell it to me. When I mentioned this to Ardith, she loved the idea of pooling our resources and seeing what we could do. She said, "Lizzy, this is just what we've been waiting for."

At this time, Ardith and I had been working together for about a year as consultants to nonprofit organizations and realized we would be better able to scale our business if we offered a product rather than a service. I was on the lookout for a product that people wanted but could not find easily. Ardith wanted to develop an internet business.

A couple of months later, Ardith and I flew to New York, signed a contract, and arranged to have the "business" shipped to my house. A few weeks later, a big brown truck delivered four large boxes stuffed with photocopied order forms, plastic bags, gold labels, a package sealer, stale candy, catalogs telling us where we could buy the fresh product, and a list of satisfied customers. We were the proud, happy, and clueless owners of Licorice International, a business that would require all our experience, expertise, and energy, plus God's continuing guidance as we navigated the uncharted waters of entrepreneurship in the age of Internet commerce.

All this happened in 2002 and we worked in the business for the next 17 years. Every Monday morning, we met with the owner of our candy store to get our orders—and not for candy—for the week. Who, you might ask, was the owner? The Lord Jesus Christ, of course.

From the start of our partnership, Ardith and I agreed that God owned the business and we worked for Him. At each Monday meeting, we wrote down our concerns for the week, talked about them, prayed for direction, and trusted God to take care of His business.

During those years, we didn't always agree, but we never argued. If one of us didn't feel confident about a decision, we didn't move forward. Sometimes being stuck in these crossroads wasn't easy, but we agreed early on that the value of our friendship far outweighed the value of the business.

Of course, we had our share of ups and downs. Like the roof collapsing in the middle of a busy summer tourist season and two burglaries where we lost several hundred dollars. In one

GOD'S GIFT OF SMELL
— Eryn Lynum —

SALT PERMEATES AN OCEAN'S WATER and the breeze passing over it, as the blowing air picks up and carries salt particles. The briny aroma is immediately noticeable and can be surprising to someone unaccustomed to it.

Matthew 5:13 (NIV) says, "You are the salt of the earth." Christ calls His believers to serve the same purpose in the spiritual world that salt performs in our daily lives: enhancing and flavoring everything with goodness while preserving truth and pushing back decay. Like someone standing at the ocean's edge and inhaling its unmistakable salty aroma, a person in the proximity of Christ's followers should immediately sense a difference, or, as 2 Corinthians 2:15 (NIV) calls it, "the pleasing aroma of Christ."

---

case, the thief was apprehended quickly, because, in addition to taking our money, he also stole a tub of licorice, which the police found in his motel room. Even worse than losing our money, the breach shattered our sense of security. Through this experience, we realized that depending on God also meant being wise. We soon set up a much better security system.

As the seasons of our lives changed we prepared to hand off the business to a new owner. For 3 years we asked God to lead us to the right person. I can't say we waited patiently but we waited. We rejoiced when an employee who had worked for us for nearly

15 years expressed interest in buying the company. We sold it to her in June 2019 and have never looked back.

Since then, Ardith and I have remained best friends and prayer partners. Together, we've weathered the pandemic, our husbands' health issues, family challenges, and the travails of aging. After all these years, we still talk on the phone daily, pray together every week, work on mission projects at church, and, of course, keep our eyes open for God's next great adventure.

God's Faithfulness to Lead Us

Lisa Lenning

We followed the realtor's car up a steep and winding road, through a community of homes in Western North Carolina called Mountain Valley. A thunderstorm had recently moved through the area, but the sun was starting to shine as we pulled into the driveway of the house for sale.

"Let's make this quick, okay? I want to get on the road to visit your mom in Greensboro. We still have over a 3-hour drive," I murmured to my husband.

We almost canceled the house visit due to the storm that morning. It seemed like a waste of time since we were only researching potential areas for a future move. We did not have a plan to sell our house in Illinois, where we lived and raised our kids for over 20 years. However, we'd been praying for God's direction in our next phase as empty nesters. The trip to Western North Carolina, then to visit family in Greensboro, was the beginning of the research process.

In recent years, God had planted the seed of a dream in our hearts to one day own a home for hosting missionaries' and pastors' families. We regularly supported Christian mission work internationally and in the US through our Illinois church, and recently increased our financial giving to mission work. My husband's parents had served as missionaries in Cameroon years ago, and his father had pastored several Lutheran churches in the US as well. We hoped to someday serve pastors and missionaries by offering them a place of rest and respite.

Ed, the real estate agent, met us at the front door. But just as he put his key in the lockbox, the door opened unexpectedly.

A stylish woman in her early 70s greeted us with a warm smile.

"Welcome! I'm Betsy, the owner. I hope you don't mind that I stayed home. Our power went out from the storm and I wanted to be sure I could show you around with a flashlight if necessary. But thank goodness the power just went back on! I can leave if you want to look around without me."

Ed glanced at us questioningly. Most Realtors prefer to show a house without the owners present.

"No, that's fine. We are good with you being here," my husband said.

> **Jesus immediately reached out his hand and took hold of him, saying to him, "O you of little faith, why did you doubt?"**
>
> —MATTHEW 14:31 (ESV)

From the moment we stepped inside the house, we had a sense that God was speaking to us.

The entryway and vaulted living room area boasted large windows facing the Blue Ridge Mountains.

"Wow. That view is amazing!" I said.

"Yes, we love it. God gives us a different sunset over the mountains to enjoy every night. And you see that peak in the distance? That's Mount Pisgah," Betsy explained.

Mount Pisgah? I'd just read about this very mountain peak in my daily Bible reading plan. God took Moses to the top of Pisgah and showed him the Promised Land (Deuteronomy 34). Was this a coincidence or was God saying something to us?

After touring the upper level, which already piqued our interest, Betsy said, "Wait until you see the lower level!"

We followed her through a door off the laundry room, down a staircase to a fully furnished apartment, complete with three bedrooms, two full bathrooms, a small kitchen, and a dining and living area.

"The original owner had this home built specifically for housing missionaries and their families. There is even a separate entrance and driveway. He was very involved in his church missions. I believe several missionary families stayed here while he and his wife owned the home."

Our jaws dropped.

"Ed, did you know this?" I exclaimed.

"No ma'am, I did not."

Ed later told us he almost dropped to his knees in awe of God at that moment. When my husband and I first met with Ed, we shared about our family background and our dream of owning a home for missionaries' and pastors' families.

Then Betsy told us they'd had an offer on the house a few months ago, but it had fallen through unexpectedly. She and her husband had been praying for just the right family to purchase their home.

"I think God sent you to be the next owners!" she said with a smile.

We walked out to our car in a state of shock. What had just happened? It seemed crazy, yet my husband and I both sensed God was leading us to make an offer on the house. But the timing was not at all according to our plan. Besides, I felt emotionally unprepared to sell our home in Illinois and leave our dear friends and church family. How would our young adult children, some who were still finishing college, manage without us living nearby? And how would we afford to own two homes until our Illinois house sold?

Then I recalled a prayer I'd journaled a few days earlier. After reading how the Israelites lacked faith and trust in God to enter the promised land (Numbers 14), I wrote this prayer: "Oh Lord, forgive me for my lack of faith. Increase my faith in You!"

It seemed God was answering my prayer.

After praying together and seeking wise counsel, my husband and I believed God was leading us, and we needed to trust Him. We made an offer on the home 2 days later. The owners accepted, and the journey began.

After the initial step of faith, I confess I experienced times of fear and doubt. I was reminded of the story of Peter in Matthew 14:29–31, how he began to sink in the water after initially stepping out of the boat to meet Jesus. Fear and uncertainty over the future caused me to sink and want to turn back. In the months before our house in Illinois sold, I struggled with doubt that we were actually following God's lead.

> **Trust in the LORD with all your heart, and do not lean on your own understanding. In all your ways acknowledge him, and he will make straight your paths.**
>
> —PROVERBS 3:5–6 (ESV)

But just as Jesus reached out to Peter in his distress, He reassured me through His Word and wise counsel that He would remain faithful to us, even when the journey was hard and uncertain.

And God was faithful beyond our expectations! We were able to cover the cost of our house payments until our Illinois home sold. Our adult children gradually adjusted and grew in maturity through the transition process. And even though I struggled to leave my friends and family, God gave me the daily courage and strength that I needed. Eleven months after we said "Yes!" to God's unexpected call to move, we loaded up our moving van to follow God's leading to a new adventure in North Carolina.

> Make me to know your ways, O LORD; teach me your paths. Lead me in your truth and teach me, for you are the God of my salvation; for you I wait all the day.
>
> —PSALM 25:4–5 (ESV)

As I reflect on that time 4 years later, I clearly see that God's plan and timing was better than my own understanding. Moving had its challenges, and at times I felt very lonely, but those times brought me closer to God in prayer. Above all, God was faithful to the vision He gave us to provide a home and retreat to missionaries and pastors.

Our first family came to stay in January of 2020, right before the pandemic hit. A young pastor named Adam and his wife and three small girls had recently moved to our area in obedience to God's call to start a college retreat ministry. They needed a place to live and happened to mention that to our neighbor at a local coffee shop. What a divine appointment! They became family to us during the 8 months they lived in our home, especially as we navigated the pandemic together. We served in aspects of their retreat ministry, and Pastor Adam officiated the wedding of our daughter in September 2020.

From that first family, God sent a steady stream of pastors, missionaries, and other guests to stay in our Mountain Rest home: married pastors from North Dakota grieving a miscarriage; a Korean pastor and his family from Illinois seeking rest after a difficult season at their church; a Filipino pastor, his wife, and daughter seeking ministry support through area churches; a cousin and pastor studying to be a chaplain and enrolled at the local VA hospital. The list goes on.

And beyond that, we have hosted Thanksgiving and Christmas gatherings, and a reunion for our children and extended family. We see over and over how God prepared the way for us to move, and how He uses our home to bless others.

I believe God is actively working all around us, and wants to lead and guide us, if we genuinely seek Him. Even when our faith starts to slip or we feel afraid, God can use mustard seed faith—those moments that seem tiny but can have a mountain-moving impact on others—to work in amazing ways. When we keep our eyes on Him, He promises to make straight our paths.

God's Guiding Hand to a Home

Laurie Herlich

For 7 years, I did not have my own address. I cleaned houses, pet-sat, and sofa-surfed. Many times, I didn't know where I would sleep the next night, but God always provided, and I never had to sleep in my car. Over and over my faith was stretched to nearly the breaking point.

There was a time in my life when things were going quite well. I was single but moving up in my career. I bought a condominium and a nice little car. Looking back, I think I was grateful to God for these blessings, but I might have secretly believed I'd achieved this relative success through my own intelligence and my own hard work.

Then things were not going well. A series of health challenges followed the dot-com crash. I lost my full-time job and couldn't find another. I had to surrender the title to my little condo back to the bank. I worked all sorts of odd jobs to have food and gas money. In between pet-sitting jobs, there were friends with whom I could stay. I traveled with a night-light so I could find my way in unfamiliar homes.

I continued to avidly job hunt and had many fruitless interviews. As time went on, I became more frightened and insecure. I wondered simultaneously if God really loved me, how could this be happening, and why I believed myself to be any more worthy than believers around the world who were starving or living under persecution. My heart ached and I shed many a tear. I learned ever so much about persevering in prayer.

After those 7 lean years, the Lord provided a full-time job and a house to rent with a longtime friend. My gratitude and relief were overwhelming. I took nothing for granted. This time I knew that it was God's provision, not my own abilities. I never wanted to repeat those years of insecurities, but I wouldn't have traded what I learned about God for any amount of security.

My friend and I worked hard and saved. We prayed for wisdom about the future as retirement loomed and costs where we were living increased faster than our salaries. We researched costs of living in many places, income and sales tax levels, and climates. More than that research, though, we prayed. I had learned that relying on my own wisdom was far substandard to God's leading and provision.

After 7 years of working and praying, we were able to move across the country. We rented a farmhouse the owners hoped to sell. My friend retired, and I found a job. We knew God had brought us to this place. The Lord led us to a Bible study where we met friends who were also committed to following Jesus and to a church where God's Word is esteemed highly. My friend got involved with a local foodbank, and I found a

> **My people will abide in a peaceful habitation, in secure dwellings, and in quiet resting places.**
>
> —ISAIAH 32:18 (ESV)

community of writers. The rain fell freely here, the hills were green and lovely. We knew we were home.

Then the Covid-19 pandemic arrived. What a blessing that my new company had a government contract and didn't have to shut down. I was able to continue working. We were beyond grateful, especially with all the unknowns the pandemic brought.

Halfway through the pandemic, while at a birthday party for the daughter of one of our friends from the Bible study, we received a phone call from our rental's property manager. He told us that our landlord was fed up with the policies of the state in which they were living and wanted to come home. To our home! Our rental agreement gave us 60 days to move.

My legs gave way and I found myself sitting on the floor. My heart sank to my toes, and I could hardly breathe.

Our friends prayed with us, and we left the party in disbelief. How could this be happening?

The next morning, my friend and I prayed together and began house-hunting in earnest. Rentals were in short supply; both apartments and houses were being snapped up, sight unseen, and prices were skyrocketing. It seemed that everyone wanted to flee the big cities with their dense populations and accompanying high risk of contracting Covid.

My retired housemate perused the Internet all day, making appointments for places to visit. By the time I got home from work, though, the rentals had already been by people who offered to pay extra. After 2 weeks of repeated disappointments, our spirits were heavy.

Desperate times called for desperate measures. My housemate had a great credit rating. I had been avoiding credit since my period of involuntary joblessness—never again did I want to be caught with bills I couldn't pay—so I didn't have much of a credit rating. However, my thriftiness meant I had cash savings. We doubled our prayers and asked for God's guidance. My friend and I agreed that if we were turned down for a loan, it would be a sign this was not the correct direction to go, and we would continue to look for rentals.

Armed with this resolve, we went to the credit union. We qualified for a loan and had enough for a down payment! Our hopes soared, causing a moment of dancing as we left the credit union. Surely, we believed, God was blessing our endeavor.

There was a small catch though. Escrow usually lasts 45 days, and we were well into our 60 days' notice. Would we have to erode our savings by putting our belongings in storage, staying in a motel, and then moving out of storage into a new residence?

> **For you are my rock and my fortress; and for your name's sake you lead and guide me.**
>
> —PSALM 31:3 (ESV)

The next morning, before I left for work, we prayed with renewed vigor, asking God for His guidance. Searching for homes to buy was not much more encouraging than hunting for rentals. We didn't qualify for a large loan and prices were rising. As with rentals, people were purchasing properties sight unseen over the Internet.

Where could we go? What could we do?

That weekend we spent every minute looking online and making appointments to see places to purchase or rent.

On Saturday, at the first house, I recoiled from entering. Even the doorstep was crawling with roaches. The next was leaning out over a hillside. If I had a marble, it would've rolled straight to the other side of the house and up the wall. The following appointment sent us a cancellation text as we pulled in the driveway.

Sunday after church brought more disappointment. One house reeked of mildew. The next house was multilevel with stairs everywhere, and I was still healing from a severe ankle injury. The following residence required many expensive repairs. The coup de grace was another cancellation.

> **Out of my distress I called on the LORD; the LORD answered me and set me free.**
>
> —PSALM 118:5 (ESV)

We pulled into a parking lot. I collapsed into tears, crying hysterically. I begged God, "I just cannot be homeless again!" I cried until there were no more tears, and we drove back to the farmhouse dejectedly.

I turned in early. I had to be ready to go back to work the following day. I was exhausted.

My housemate was not to be discouraged. At half past 9, I was summoned to come back to the living room. A house that had not been listed 10 minutes earlier was now visible.

It was just the right size and price, in a neighborhood that I loved and had driven through many times. I whispered, "Please, God, could there be a home for us here?" We studied the photos of the house, inside and out.

"It's now or never," I said. We prayed quickly and fervently.

Our real estate agent was on vacation in Myrtle Beach but helped us submit our bid just before midnight—yes, sight unseen.

Monday, the agent's partner arranged for us to tour the house. It was being shown every 20 minutes the entire day!

By the end of the day, the owner later told us she had five solid bids, most higher than ours. As she prayed, she kept pushing our bid aside in favor of the higher bids, but God kept leading her back to ours.

In the end, our bid was selected. We still had to make it through closing before time was up on our rental agreement, but the Lord took care of that as well. Inspections, repairs, and paperwork all came together in record time. We signed and moved the same day. All professionals involved were amazed at how quickly it went through. It truly was a miracle.

It was God's miracle, not our efforts that gave us a home. He hears our prayers of faith and answers, in His own time and His own way. Sometimes it takes 7 years; sometimes it takes 2 agonizing weeks. We did not deserve a home—it was unmerited favor, like grace, like the gift of salvation through Jesus Christ.

The Gift of a Slow Elevator

Sandy Kirby Quandt

The sun rose to my right, filling the sky with glorious color. If only I felt as full of promise as the horizon looked. I was headed to a writer's conference early that October morning. Another conference. Another time when I questioned whether writing was what God wanted me to do. I felt this might truly be my last one. After attending numerous conferences for multiple years, studying, and applying what I'd learned to my writing, I didn't seem to be any closer to my dream of becoming a published author than when I first started this quest. I was discouraged. Was it time to be realistic and give up my dream?

About 50 minutes later, the tall buildings of downtown Houston came into view. Beltway traffic slowed in the usual spots. Cars cut each other off as they maneuvered toward their exits. Horns blared. And just as predictably, I prayed for God's clear direction regarding my writing.

"Father, I'm confused. I thought writing was something You wanted me to do. Now I'm not so sure. I believe You placed a love of writing in me. Lately, though, I'm questioning if it is what You want me to do. Did I hear You wrong? Please show me how You want me to proceed. Make it plain so there is no room for doubt. Are You telling me to quit or are You telling me to keep writing? I don't know. Is writing Your plan for me, or is it merely a childhood dream?"

A billboard rose off to the side of the interstate. It advertised expert legal advice for car accidents. "Father, if You wrote the answer to my writing question on a billboard, that would help."

I sighed, tightened my grip on the steering wheel, and paid close attention to the exit signs. I wasn't far from where I needed to get off the interstate and didn't want to miss my turn. Downtown Houston is an easy place for me to get lost. It's something I've done more than once.

Today I would attend workshops with other aspiring authors learning the craft of writing. The main speaker was a well-known Christian author. I'd heard her speak one other time. I looked forward to hearing her speak again. Her words encouraged me then, and I hoped they would encourage me now.

> **If any of you lacks wisdom, you should ask God, who gives generously to all without finding fault, and it will be given to you.**
>
> —JAMES 1:5 (NIV)

After reaching the church where the conference was being held, I prayed once more. "Father, please make it clear—without a doubt. Show me how You want me to proceed. Please. Should I keep writing or quit? Thank You for going before me in this and preparing the way."

I gathered my belongings and entered the building. I followed the signs through the winding halls directing me to the area where the conference would be held. Up ahead, I saw the conference's main speaker. A little starstruck, I approached the elevator where she stood.

"Hi. My name's Sandy."

She smiled and extended her hand. "DiAnn Mills."

"I want to thank you for the keynote speech you gave on David at the conference in Dallas. I still remember it. You reminded us that God kept David tending sheep for years before He allowed David to become king. You told us not to get discouraged with God's timing in our writing. I try to remember that whenever I think things are moving too slow."

> I call on you, my God, for you will answer me; turn your ear to me and hear my prayer.
>
> —PSALM 17:6 (NIV)

"That's so sweet. Thank you for remembering what I said." DiAnn looked from me to the closed elevator door. "I'm wondering if something is wrong with the elevator. I've stood here several minutes waiting for it to arrive."

I noticed the rolling cart at her feet. "Would you like me to help carry your cart up the stairs?"

She shook her head. "No, thanks. The elevator should arrive soon."

While we waited for the very slow elevator, DiAnn and I talked about an upcoming conference she was directing. We talked about speakers we both knew who would be there. We even talked about the weather. DiAnn asked where I lived. After I told her, she looked at me a few moments as if contemplating something important.

"I lead a writer's critique group at my church once a month. It's on the other side of Houston. It'd be a drive for you. But would you like to join us?"

There it was. The confirmation I prayed for. Confirmation to keep writing and not give up.

"Thank you. I would love to join your group."

Not only did I thank DiAnn for her invitation, but I thanked God for it as well.

DiAnn reached into her bag. "Here's my card. Send me an email. I'll let you know where the church is. What time. Which day we meet. All the details."

"Thank you so much. I look forward to it."

> **The one who calls you is faithful, and he will do it.**
>
> —1 THESSALONIANS 5:24 (NIV)

As soon as I finished speaking, the elevator arrived. DiAnn and I looked at each other and laughed. She stepped inside. "I'll see you during the conference."

When the elevator door closed, I felt God had given me His clear direction for my writing. I had no doubt He used DiAnn and a slow elevator to provide an answer to my prayers. Through our chance encounter as we waited for an elevator God delayed, I knew God was in the details. He was the one who arranged the timing for me to walk down the hall at the exact moment DiAnn stood at the elevator.

There was no question God placed her in my path. Or that He made a way for us to have uninterrupted time for our conversation. God nudged DiAnn to invite me to join her critique group. He used her to encourage me not to give up. Without her knowing it, God used DiAnn to guide me on the next step of the writing path He planned for me to take.

The sun was setting late that afternoon as I drove home from the conference. The day ended as it began—full of promise. I wasn't exactly sure how God would use my writing for Him, but I did know He didn't want me to give up. Perhaps, just as tending sheep was part of God's plan for David all those years ago, attending conferences is part of God's plan for me now. Writing is my long-held dream. And I believe God used a slow elevator and a fellow writer to make clear it is also His dream.

Roots, home, neighborhood and community—these are the geographies of our lives, the places where God dwells.

—Diana Butler Bass

CHAPTER 2

The Joy of Family and Friends

Standing Under My Parents' Legacy.............68
   Lynne Hartke

When Love Brings You Home...................74
   Debbie Dueck

Country Love................................81
   Elsa Kok Colopy

A Change of Plans..........................85
   Felicia Harris-Russell

Uncharted Waters, Unchanging God.............89
   Tina Savant Gibson

A Small Breeze and A Couple of Winks.........94
   Sandra G. Beck

Divine Appointment..........................99
   Becky Hofstad

A Friend for the Write Time................105
   Bettie Boswell

Standing Under My Parents' Legacy

Lynne Hartke

I wasn't interested in returning to my hometown of Albert Lea, Minnesota, where my parents had lived for 55 years. They had both died from cancer, first my dad, followed by my mom 9 months later. I had not been back since their funerals 3 years earlier. I didn't see the point in stirring up grief and old memories.

But when I was invited to speak at my parents' church, I decided to make the most of the opportunity. I scheduled a book signing and several other speaking events, including an opening speech at a cancer walk in memory of our parents. My sisters, Renae and Lisa, made plans to join me, as did our Uncle Glenn and Aunt Cindy. Even as I organized the full weekend, I wondered how I would face all the memories.

On our first morning in Albert Lea, we decided to drive over and see our childhood home. The corn surrounding the 3 acres was not yet over my head. Memories returned of scooter rides down the hill, family reunions, and hide-and-seek under the honeysuckle bushes when we were kids.

I expected it to be difficult, this stepping closer to our birthplace. As we drove past the trees our dad had planted years before, now tall enough to shade the garden shed I had painted as a teen, I did not feel the biting pain of grief, only nostalgia.

Later we pondered our lack of intense grief on our return.

"Perhaps it is because Mom left so easily," Lisa said. She had witnessed our mother's packing and leaving after our father's death. She paused. "No, *easily* is *not* the right word."

"Bravely," Aunt Cindy said, who was with us as we processed.

"Yes," Lisa exclaimed, leaning closer to the truth in the conversation. "*Bravely* is the word."

After Dad's death, Mom had loaded four suitcases representing 78 years of life into my sister's car to catch a flight to live with us in Arizona.

I knew this part of the story.

But my sister shared a deeper story. Lisa remembered saying goodbye to the house and driving past the harvested cornfields. They drove through Albert Lea, the town where I grew up, before hitting the freeway and heading north toward the airport in Minneapolis. Mom had talked matter-of-factly to Lisa while saying her goodbyes to her old home, embracing whatever God had in front of her.

> **You will be blessed in the city and blessed in the country.... You will be blessed when you come in and blessed when you go out.**
>
> —DEUTERONOMY 28:3, 6 (NIV)

Then a worship song came on the radio, a song of blessing God in all circumstances, even during hard times.

"Oh, I love this song," Mom had said.

"Me too," Lisa replied, still choking back a few tears. Lisa had moved away years ago, but with Mom leaving for good, Lisa was realizing that there would be few opportunities to return. It was a farewell for her too. She cranked the volume and together they sang the song of surrender. By the time they hit the final verse about failing strength and choosing praise when the end draws near, my mom and sister were belting out the lyrics at the top of their lungs.

"Bless the Lord," they sang. "I will bless the Lord."

Now, years later, the echo of that surrender continued as my sisters and I headed to the book signing at a local coffee shop. To be honest, I wasn't that excited about hosting a book signing. I had participated in signings before—often boring events where I tried to convince strangers to buy books. Too often, people shuffled past my table as quickly as possible as they tried to avoid making eye contact.

> **Praise the Lord, my soul; all my inmost being, praise his holy name. Praise the Lord, my soul, and forget not all his benefits.**
>
> —PSALM 103:1–2 (NIV)

Besides that, I knew I was basically a stranger in my own hometown. I had come back almost every year to visit my parents, but had not lived in Albert Lea since I had graduated from high school. My expectations for anyone coming to the book signing were low.

"If nobody shows up," Renae said as she organized books on the table, "we can still visit and order food."

"True," I said. "The pumpkin muffins look delicious. And I would love an iced tea."

"I need coffee," Lisa exclaimed as she lugged in another box of books. "Lots. Of. Coffee."

Still laughing, we had no time to order that needed coffee before the bell over the door jingled. Janet walked in, a mother of one of my high school friends—and much more than that. When Mom had been in rehab after a stroke, Janet had driven to the facility every night to read a devotion with Mom at the close of the day.

While I was still chatting with Janet, an older man walked in.

"You won't remember me," he boomed, "but I was your dad's teaching partner." As I handed him a signed copy, Dad's old hunting buddy shuffled through the door.

Lisa offered me an iced tea as the man who had once owned the Mobile gas station introduced himself. He had hired Dad 50 years earlier when my parents first moved to Albert Lea. As a new teacher, with a young family, Dad needed the additional income. For several years, Dad worked weekends and evenings pumping gas.

> One generation commends your works to another; they tell of your mighty acts.
>
> —PSALM 145:4 (NIV)

The bell on the door jingled again. My sixth-grade teacher walked into the room, followed by my tenth-grade creative writing teacher. Soon, they were joined by the man who introduced me to my husband. Right behind him stood our wedding photographer.

I had barely finished greeting the new arrivals when three women showed up who had organized a baby shower for our oldest son before we had moved to Arizona. They pulled out pictures of their great-grandchildren and cooed over photos of our grandchildren.

GOD'S GIFT OF TOUCH
— Kimberly Shumate —

RUNNERS PAY A LOT OF attention to their shoes, because the constant impact of feet on ground can wear down a sole and injure their bodies in unexpected ways. The same is true of our souls. How often do we feel the hard, unyielding ground beneath our feet as we run a race of challenges and uncertainty? Though our flesh has its limits, our God has none. "He remembers that we are dust" (Psalm 103:14, NIV) and will gently lift us up when the journey becomes too much. Though our earthly struggles leave temporary scars, God's impression is everlasting—His beauty mark is eternal.

"Oh, how time flies," they exclaimed one after the other. "We remember attending church with your folks when you all were little. You sat in the pew in matching dresses, along with your brother." Lifelong friends, they shared stories of the evening Bible study they had attended with Dad and Mom for over thirty years.

For the next 3 hours, people arrived and told stories of generations of shared life. The afternoon turned out to be nothing like I had imagined or feared. We listened to those who still stood as witnesses to our parents' lives. As I gazed around the room, I realized many of these gray-haired men and women had prayed for me since I was a child.

My mom left Albert Lea, Minnesota, with a song on her lips about blessing God in all circumstances. That blessing linked us to this community. We did not stand alone as strangers. We were connected to generations, beyond the scope of time. Although Mom and Dad were not with us in that room, I knew my siblings and I still stood under the blessing of our parents' legacy.

When Love Brings You Home

Debbie Dueck

"Debbie, come with me. I need to tell you a secret."

I followed my 94-year-old aunt down the paneled hallway of her mobile home to her bedroom. I pinched my arm. *Was this happening? What was she going to tell me that I didn't already know?*

Painful childhood experiences stood like a wall between my father and his two sisters, preventing them from a meaningful relationship. Blame and accusatory words fired back and forth in their letters, deepening resentment. Occasionally, a crack would appear in the form of friendliness but never enough to knock the wall down. As they aged, I prayed earnestly for reconciliation.

I knew some fragmentary details of my father's troubled early years. His mother, wearing her "going-out" black dress and a string of pearls, took one last peek at her three sleeping young children and walked out, never to return. It was 1925. Devastated, Grandpa did his best as a single father, but his children needed a mother. Seven years later, he remarried, hoping to establish his dream family. Though they began attending church faithfully, more trouble ensued.

Hungry for a mother's love, my father quickly became his stepmother's favorite, which made life unbearable for the preteen girls. Vivian, with developmental challenges, stayed and endured, but not Evie. She finished high school early and ran away before turning eighteen, breaking her father's heart. Eventually, she made her whereabouts known but never returned home.

Growing up, Dad called Evie the "black sheep" of the family. "She knows the way, but she's not following it," he would say.

In my adult years, I wondered why Evie never returned home. Could there be more to her story? After my father and Vivian passed away, I prayed more earnestly that Evie would know God's peace before it was too late. In 2016, an intense urge stirred in my heart to visit her in person. She lived in Wisconsin. I lived in California. I tried to reason with God—it was too far, too expensive, and too many years had passed. Yet I couldn't shake the prompting. My son, an airline agent, arranged standby tickets. *Okay, Lord. I'll take that as a sign if I get a seat on the plane.*

I'd seen Evie a couple of times over the years, but never for long and never very often. I wondered if she'd even remember me. I called her, asking if she'd like a visit.

"Yes! Please come!" I could hear Evie smiling through the phone.

Hearing my name called for a standby seat at the airline gate assured me my urge was meant to be. *I'm going in obedience, Lord. I leave the results to You.*

I knew Evie lived alone on a lot at Lake Lawrence. She had no family nearby, only her rambunctious dog, Kibbie, to keep her company and a few Good Samaritan neighbors. Butterflies danced in my stomach as I drove into her driveway, finding myself transported back to 1974. We'd stopped here on vacation. I was seventeen then. Evie had just married Art, the divorced father of ten children—a marriage never approved by Grandpa or Dad.

How should I greet her? Will we recognize each other after forty-two years?

> **The Spirit of the Lord is upon me, because he has anointed me to proclaim good news to the poor. He has sent me to proclaim liberty to the captives and recovering of sight to the blind, to set at liberty those who are oppressed.**
>
> —LUKE 4:18 (ESV)

Excited barking announced my arrival as I opened the car door. A slightly stooped lady with white shoulder-length hair opened her screen door and walked toward me. Her small white dog ran circles around my legs.

"Hello! Aunt Evie." I patted her shoulder. "It's good to see you."

"I know." Though she was aged, the chuckle in her voice hadn't changed. "I've been waiting for your visit. I'm sorry I didn't dress up better."

Wearing black slacks, a pink-and-white-striped blouse that could've used a fresh wash, and sports shoes larger than her size, she looked good for a 94-year-old.

"You look fine." I bit my lip, fighting emotion. *Am I really here?*

"Come in."

I followed her into the deteriorating mobile home so thick with dust and dog hair they made you sneeze.

"Here's Art's picture with our dog. I think it's good. I took it."

"It is a good picture," I agreed, glancing around. I saw no pictures of her birth family or Art's kids—only her with Art and their pets.

"Art was a good man. He took care of me. That's all I wanted." She reached out and grabbed my hand.

"Come. I need to tell you a secret."

Completely taken by surprise, I followed down the hall to her bedroom, having no idea about the essence of her buried secret, crying for release.

We sat on her faded blue floral bedspread.

"You know Goldie, my stepmother, was mean to Vivian and me. She beat me so badly that I had to wear long stockings to cover up my bruised legs. Sometimes, she'd even lock me up in the closet."

Looking into her faded gray eyes that showed no pretense, I didn't see a black sheep. I saw a wounded little girl.

"That's horrible," I sympathized.

Painful memories began spilling out so fast that her dentures became dislodged, forcing her to reset them as she talked.

"My folks had a small corner grocery store where I worked in my teens. I never got paid a single dime. One day my tongue got all twisted up. I said a word to Goldie that I didn't mean. I really didn't! I tried to explain. She wouldn't listen. She slapped

> **God was reconciling the world to himself in Christ, not counting people's sins against them. And he has committed to us the message of reconciliation.**
>
> —2 CORINTHIANS 5:19 (NIV)

me with a wet dish towel across the face and threatened to send me away. Terrified, I ran away to the safety of friends."

My heart felt stabbed.

She continued. "I got an office job at a trucking company and joined a bowling league. Life was good. I was content. One Friday evening after work, I went bowling as usual. My coworker was gone for the weekend visiting her ailing mother. When I left the bowling alley, I noticed my coworker's husband waiting by my car. *Odd*, I thought. I was naive. He coerced me into his car, drove me to his house, and raped me."

"Raped you?" My jaw dropped. "Oh, Evie, I'm so sorry. I never knew." *Why had I never heard this?* Tears filled my eyes. I placed my hand gently on her shoulder.

> **There is no fear in love. But perfect love drives out fear because fear has to do with punishment. The one who fears is not made perfect in love.**
>
> —1 JOHN 4:18 (NIV)

"No, I suppose you didn't. Goldie had never told me anything about sex, about men. Nothing."

Gut-wrenching. Sixty years had passed yet this gnawing secret was as fresh as yesterday.

"I learned I was pregnant."

"Pregnant!" I caught my breath, imagining being illegitimately pregnant in the 1950s.

"What did you do?"

"I quit my job and moved to a home for unwed mothers in Milwaukee." She paused. "I gave birth to a baby boy."

"You did?" *Unbelievable.* "Then what?"

"A young couple adopted him. I never met them. I heard they were nice. I held my baby once. He was a healthy boy."

I gathered my aunt in my arms and cradled her close like a child, hoping my embrace would soothe the pain. She leaned in. My tears spilled down and landed on her hair. She relaxed. How incredulous that God allowed me to be the one to hear her dark confession. I knew, without a doubt, that God had designed this moment. I admired her courageous decision to give life to a child, conceived not in love but conceived just the same.

"Do you think I did the right thing?" she whispered.

"Oh, yes!" I patted her shoulder.

"You think so?" Her voice barely above a whisper.

"I know so! You did nothing wrong in that situation. And for all our mistakes, Jesus forgives us when we ask Him. He loves you so much. You did the best thing. You gave a little boy the chance to show the world the gifts God has given to him. And someday we'll learn all about it. It will be amazing."

"You're right." Evie lifted her head. "For a while now, I've been reading a chapter in the Bible and praying before I go to bed. It makes me feel good. Like God is with me."

Hallelujah! He was answering my prayers.

"Your family endured many difficult things," I said, looking directly into her eyes, visualizing her and my father and Vivian. "We'll never understand why your mother abandoned you. God never did. God has always watched over you and your family. He loves you. I know they're waiting in heaven for you."

"That'll be nice." Evie gave a little chuckle. "I'll be ninety-five years old in September. I often wonder, why does God still have me here?"

"I think it was so I could come and see you."

She smiled. "It's so good to talk to someone who understands. I'm glad you came!"

"Me too. I love you, Aunt Evie. I'm glad we're family."

"We are more than family. We are friends."

Four months later, one of Evie's neighbors called to let me know Evie was gone. I grieved and rejoiced, thanking God that I listened to His prompting and obeyed. I shudder to imagine my regret if I hadn't. Oh, the joy of reconciliation! I know Evie is rejoicing with her Savior, Jesus, and her family. Reunited. Reconciled. Evie is forever home.

Country Love
Elsa Kok Colopy

We couldn't have been more different. Esther was a former Amish woman in her mid-70s, and I was a young single mom in my 20s. Esther was always conservatively dressed and well put-together, her blouses buttoned up to her chin and tucked into fancy slacks or lovely gingham skirts. Her hair was always perfectly coiffed for every occasion. I preferred sweatshirts and cozy jeans and windswept hair pulled up into a ponytail.

I'm not sure why Esther loved me, but she did. I met her at a divorce recovery retreat and we'd instantly connected. While she was prim and proper, she also had a great laugh and a sharp wit. We bantered back and forth about all manner of things as she wove her way into my young heart.

Esther had been married nearly 32 years when her husband left her for a younger woman. She described herself in that moment as "a piece of trash flapping in the breeze at the bottom of a garbage dump." She'd grieved and raged and healed through that heartbreak as God met her in the midst of her pain. Out of that she had come to volunteer at the retreat to help other hurting souls. For me, I'd only been married 4 years, but the situation had been beyond broken as I battled verbal abuse and multiple betrayals. To be clear, I wasn't bride of the year either. We'd been two broken people trying to fix each other. It simply didn't work.

When I first showed up at the retreat and met Esther, I was wrapped up in a lot of shame. I couldn't believe I had landed in this situation. I'd grown up in a Christian home with a loving family. I had four older brothers, three of whom were married to amazing godly women. Their children were off-the-charts adorable as well. Their families were nestled into cozy homes with delightful knickknacks and lovely decor. They were about as close to perfect as I could imagine, and I truly resented all of their wonderful choices as I sat with the consequences of my poor decisions.

> **We love because he first loved us.**
>
> —1 JOHN 4:19 (NIV)

It wasn't really fair of me. They were fine people and I was the one who needed some serious help. What was wrong with me? I felt such shame and embarrassment that I was the only one to go through a divorce.

I'd love to say that coming to the retreat was the turning point for me, but I was still looking for someone to fix the broken in me. I was trying Jesus, but I was also looking for another knight in shining armor who might be a bit better than the first one I'd chosen. In fact, just a week after the retreat, I was scheduled to be part of a dart tournament with a handsome cowboy I was getting to know.

On a whim I invited Esther to come to the tournament. I wasn't thinking, at least not clearly, about how a country bar was probably not high on her list of weekend hot spots. I just knew that I liked her and enjoyed her company.

No matter. Esther still came. I'll never forget glancing over to see her sitting with her legs crossed daintily, her hands folded gracefully on her lap. The music was thumping, the crowd was loud, and she was the picture of dignity in the midst of it all. At one point I threw a great dart. Bull's-eye! I was surprised to hear a yelp of celebration from behind me. I glanced over to see Esther on her feet.

"Good job, Elsa! Nice shot!"

Something in Esther melted me. The sheer love. The lack of judgment. The sharp wit. The kindness. Because she was willing to show up in my world, I felt like I could let her into mine. I began to seek her out more and more, talk to her about my life, let her into the shadows of my journey, and that led to a conversation that completely changed my perspective.

Esther and I were sitting outside on a warm wooden bench in the late afternoon sunshine one day, and I was bemoaning my situation once again. I turned to her in tears.

> **But God demonstrates his own love for us in this: While we were still sinners, Christ died for us.**
>
> —ROMANS 5:8 (NIV)

"Esther, I should have known better. I knew better than to marry him in the first place. I did it all wrong. I knew better than to let it all fall apart. I should have made better decisions, I should."

Esther looked at me, her blue eyes twinkling. "Elsa, stop. You have to stop 'should'-ing on yourself."

I gasped. Esther had almost cursed! She smiled broadly as she took my hands into her own.

"No more. Bring that guilt to God, ask for His forgiveness, and receive it. Then put this behind you. 'Should'-ing on yourself does no good—not for you, not for your little girl, and not for anyone you meet. It's time to let it go."

Something loosened in me that day. A weight slid off my shoulders and onto the grassy patch by our feet. No more.

I hugged my dear friend close.

I had probably heard Esther's wisdom from other people. I'd probably sat through services that spoke on forgiveness and letting go of shame. I'd probably heard about the love of Jesus a hundred different ways by then. But when prim and proper Esther showed up at a country bar to cheer me on in a dart tournament, I met Jesus. My heart was softened and that led to conversations that shaped my faith in significant ways. I'd always thought Jesus was a bearded Middle Eastern man. Turns out in that season of my life, He looked a whole lot like a woman in her 70s, prim and proper, at a country bar.

> **Whoever turns a sinner from the error of their way will save them from death and cover over a multitude of sins.**
>
> —JAMES 5:20 (NIV)

A Change of Plans
Felicia Harris-Russell

"Oh Lord!" I said as I read part of the text message from my friend Davonda. It stated that my goddaughter, Cayla, dropped a surprise bomb on her and Cayla's father, Ron. Two days prior to move-in at a 4-year university, Cayla informed her parents she no longer wanted to attend that school.

I caught my breath as I continued to read. Cayla's passion was now to become a licensed makeup artist. To train for the fulfillment of that dream, she wanted to attend a local beauty college in Georgia, and then continue her training at a renowned school in California, which was over 2,000 miles away from home. Although unspoken in the text message, I was confident that some intense moments of fellowship took place between Cayla and her parents after hearing the news of her change of plans.

I laid my cell phone on the coffee table and began praying about the situation. After prayer, my mind raced back to the joyous day when Cayla was born. When I received the text message from Davonda telling me Cayla had made her entrance into the world that morning, I didn't hesitate to drop everything and rush to the hospital. As I drove, I prayed that I wouldn't get pulled over for disregarding more than a few posted speed limits.

When I arrived, I decided to check in on Davonda first. She was doing well—a little tired and groggy, but well. Shortly after I arrived in Davonda's room, the nurse brought in Cayla, and I took her in my arms. *Wow, what a gift!* I thought. The gratitude I felt melted my heart and I choked back tears. In my arms, I held a glorious promise fulfilled—living proof of God's faithfulness, goodness, and love. There was no doubt in my mind that Cayla was the most adorable baby born in that hospital on Mother's Day. But, of course, I was more than a little biased.

The fact that Cayla was here with us, in the flesh, was more than enough. But God really outdid Himself when He allowed her to be born on Mother's Day. For any mother to give birth to a healthy, precious child on Mother's Day is truly divine. But for Davonda and Ron, it was especially sweet.

> **But he said to me, "My grace is sufficient for you, for my power is made perfect in weakness." Therefore I will boast all the more gladly of my weaknesses, so that the power of Christ may rest upon me.**
>
> —2 CORINTHIANS 12:9 (ESV)

You see, Davonda and Ron had been trying to have a baby for more than 5 years. Cayla had been the yearning of her parents' hearts for as long as I had known them. When Davonda told me that she was pregnant, I cried and shouted for joy at the same time.

As with most couples battling infertility, their pathway was not an easy or straightforward one. It was full of doubts, twists, heartbreaks, and disappointments. But they were blessed to be surrounded by a loving family and a nurturing community who prayed for them, encouraged them, and affirmed their dream every step of the way. They were not alone in their struggles.

Growing up, Cayla had always been a bright student and a kindhearted person. And she wasn't afraid to create her own path and do things that were nontraditional. I had no doubt that she would be successful no matter what career she chose to pursue. *Makeup artist,* I thought. *She'll probably formulate her own products and launch a breakthrough cosmetic line. She's just that smart.*

I have always admired the close relationship between Davonda and Cayla. I have only seen Davonda offer unconditional love and support to her daughter as she helped Cayla navigate her independence and dreams. It's because of that strong bond between mother and daughter that I knew it had to be incredibly scary and unnerving for Davonda to think of her only daughter moving by herself over 2,000 miles away from home to a place she had never been before.

> **When I am afraid, I put my trust in you.**
>
> —PSALM 56:3 (NIV)

My heart was burdened for my friend. I imagined that she had the same worries of other mothers whose children move far away from home. *What if something happens and I can't get to her fast enough?* or *"What if she gets involved with the wrong kind of people?"* If I were in that situation, I would most definitely have those concerns and more.

Davonda wrestled deeply with Cayla's decision. Many nights instead of sleeping, she was in her pajamas sending up fervent prayers for her child. And she didn't just pray for Cayla—she prayed for herself too. She prayed for God's strength and grace to carry her through. She prayed that God would help her accept Cayla's decision so that she could give her child the support she needed at this vulnerable time in her life.

In the end, Davonda accepted Cayla's decision to become a makeup artist, even though she wished that Cayla would have communicated that desire sooner. Sooner, as in before financial aid paperwork had been completed. Sooner, as in before certain school expenses had been paid. Sooner, as in before extended time-off requests were approved at work. And sooner, as in before a hundred other things had been arranged to ensure a smooth first day of college.

Several months later, I received another text message from Davonda. This time it was a happy one that showed stunning photos of Cayla's work as a student makeup artist. "Absolutely gorgeous!" I wrote back as I admired the dazzling artistry on the model's face.

> **Behold, children are a gift of the LORD, the fruit of the womb is a reward.**
>
> —PSALM 127:3 (NASB)

Davonda's pride and pleasure beamed through the words in the message. I was so proud of Cayla and Davonda.

While Davonda is at peace with Cayla's decision to become a makeup artist, she is still working on accepting Cayla's potential move to California. She's leaning into God's grace more than ever and learning anew that sometimes acceptance comes in baby steps instead of one big leap.

If I know Davonda as I think I do, while it will be heart-wrenching, she will release Cayla into God's hands—the One who gave her a cherished gift 18 years ago. And the One she can completely trust to watch over her darling daughter even when she can't.

Uncharted Waters, Unchanging God

Tina Savant Gibson

When Mama died unexpectedly, the emptiness felt unfamiliar. I tried to fill my days with busyness, but that didn't last long, for nighttime always came, inviting sadness to steal my sleep. I continued to go through the motions, faking my "fine" for fear if I allowed a glimpse of grief to sneak out, it would swallow me whole. So I sucked in my tears and leaned into survival mode. I was simply going through the motions, even at church.

During that time, we were in the middle of "group season," an opportunity to gather with others, encourage one another, pray together, and build community, usually held in someone's home. Sounds amazing, right? Well, here's the thing. I wasn't a community person. I was a mama's girl. Yet, I couldn't ignore God's supernatural nudge when the preacher asked for leaders, something that was never on my radar. My trust issues were legendary and Mama had been my safe place. Inviting women I didn't know into my home with the possibility of being vulnerable ... umm, I don't think so. Fear is so convincing. Fear is such a liar.

Later that day, my rebellion transformed into a random conversation with my husband, as I declared, "I think I'm going to lead a group!"

He smiled and said, "You mean, join a group?"

"Nope," I replied. "I want to lead one."

I'm not sure who was more surprised, him or me. It was sort of an out-of-body experience. My lips were moving, but was that really me talking? A few weeks later, my living room was filled with women of all ages and stages of life.

Truth is, I chose to hide my ache in the spotlight of community. I told myself that this group thing was a good thing, a God thing, but deep within, I had my own agenda. It included pouring His love into others while gripping my hand over my very private heart. I really believed this community stuff was more for them than for me. What I didn't count on was that my Creator Father, the one who designed me, knew me, and loved me like crazy, had other plans. Change doesn't happen overnight and that's the beauty of God's grace.

> **You will go out in joy and be led forth in peace; the mountains and hills will burst into song before you.**
>
> —ISAIAH 55:12 (NIV)

We met on Tuesday evenings at my house. As women arrived, they'd grab a snack and chat before we dug into a devotion. Right off the bat, there was one young woman who stood out. She always came at the very last minute, sweeping in the front door like a gentle wind, quickly, quietly, trying not to be noticed. But I did notice because in many ways, she reminded me of myself.

At the end of that first evening, as everyone left to re-enter their worlds, JG lingered. Week after week, she would delay her exit with a question or something totally random like "Have you ever heard of this song?" ready to play it for me on her phone.

Eventually, small talk turned into big conversations and I discovered that my group was her third attempt to connect with women through a church. She said that if this one didn't work out, she was done trying. D-O-N-E. And, when I looked into her eyes, I could tell she meant it.

When the Covid-19 pandemic paused the world a few months later, our group disbanded, but JG and I chose to be intentional. She came over to our home on Sundays, and she, my husband, and I worshiped God together. Afterward, she and I would go for a walk or bake chocolate chip cookies, something she had never done before. Sometimes we would simply sit on the floor of my office and dig into life's great mysteries. Deep questions. Hard questions. The "why" questions. And, even while missing Mama, mentoring started to heal my heart.

> **Though you have not seen him, you love him; and even though you do not see him now, you believe in him and are filled with an inexpressible and glorious joy.**
>
> —1 PETER 1:8 (NIV)

Slowly and over time, I felt a shift in my soul. It wasn't always easy. Growing pains were plentiful. I learned that freedom comes from sharing our experiences. The ones that sting. The ones that stay with us for way too long. The ones that bring hope. The ones that we're still struggling with. The ones that teach us how to love. Love. Not just those in our bloodline or our tight-knit friendship circle, but those whose paths cross our lives, whether for a season or a reason.

Then, right in the middle of my contentment, our family was presented with an opportunity to move. Not 15 minutes away—more like 15 hours away. Both my husband and I wrestled with it in our own ways, yet in the end, we were certain it was God's will. JG and I knew that God had a plan for us, too, although we couldn't see it and we didn't like it. Now, in retrospect, I can say it was a turning point in our relationship, a reminder—again—to trust our faithful Father.

About a year after the move, during one of our evening FaceTime conversations, JG wanted to talk about baptism. We had touched on that topic in the past, but this out-of-the-blue comment took me by surprise.

> **If you believe, you will receive whatever you ask for in prayer.**
>
> —MATTHEW 21:22 (NIV)

"I've been thinking about being baptized for a long time," she said. (I wanted to do cartwheels in that moment, but refrained.) Then she added, "And I want you to baptize me." I was stunned and honored and scared and full of joy. Most of all, I was in awe of God. The crazy thing is that our church was having a baptism service a few days later, at the same time she would be visiting. Coincidence? I didn't think so. I reached out to some folks and asked if we could be a part of it.

About 5 years after that precious wandering soul appeared in my doorway for our first group meeting, JG and I stood with arms around each other on the shore of the Atlantic Ocean. We walked together into the sea, toward the most gorgeous glittering sunshine on the water. The pastor took her left hand and I took her right as we baptized her in the name of the Father, the

GOD'S GIFT OF HEARING
— Kim Taylor Henry —

HEARING IS THE sense by which ears perceive sound. But many who hear do not listen. That is, they do not pay attention or give thought to what was heard. Almost 400 times in the Bible, someone is given the command to "listen." God wants His people to hear His message, yes. But most of all, He wants them to carefully listen to it, to truly pay attention, to give serious thought to, and to take appropriate action upon what has been heard—especially when it comes to the words of Jesus. As God told the disciples Peter, James, and John in Mark 9:7, "This is my Son, whom I love. Listen to him!" (NIV).

Son, and the Holy Spirit. All I remember is the joy. The deepest, most genuine joy I had experienced in a very long time. Light as a feather and bright as the morning sun. The kind that only God gives. The kind that only God is.

We may never know the impact of our existence on this planet and that's the point. It's not about us. It's about God in us. His power. His path. His presence. I firmly believe that's really why we are here on this earth. To step out of our comfort zones and trust Him. To walk through the hard stuff with eternal hope. To love bigger, better, and beyond the borders that block us from His abundant blessings. Because when we do, we just may find ourselves in the ocean of unchartered waters, hands up in hallelujah, hearts filled with unspeakable joy. Oh, how He loves.

A Small Breeze and A Couple of Winks

Sandra G. Beck

I remember my gut churning as I tried not to imagine someone bullying my first grader, but Kiki was calm and matter-of-fact in the telling. "As I took my lunch out of my lunch box, Joan took each thing away."

I asked my daughter, "So, what did you do?"

"I just looked at her like you look at me sometimes and said, 'Joan, give it back.' And she did!"

More than 10 years later I now sit at a summer welcome on a state university campus, wondering for the thousandth time how I could possibly release my freshman daughter into the wild. Gifted with a few minutes alone, I wander into the lounge of the beautiful, historic Memorial Union building and drop into a chair that faces an open window. Staring through the leaves of one of the old maples that keep guard out front, I take in the buildings and students and sunshine and whisper, "How can I leave her here in the fall?"

A small breeze rustles the leaves, moves through the window, and gently caresses my face. It feels so still and yet so strong in my heart, as the Spirit says to me, "I am here, and I will be with her." I believe Him . . . mostly.

You might think this story is about my daughter and her journey through academia. It is not. It's about me—a fearful, worried, oh-ye-of-little-faith mom who couldn't imagine the size of my God and His ability to craft my daughter's experience to build my faith and give me a deeper trust in Him and what He can do.

Fall arrived and with nothing to do as parents but trust the Spirit's quiet, strong voice, we moved Kiki into her dorm. Boxes and stairs and fraternity boys helping with carts and then meeting her new roommate along with her dad. As the girls worked out who would take which bed and which closet each would claim, my husband and I talked with her dad. It wasn't long before he said, "Are you all Christ-followers?" We learned that he was a science professor on campus and was involved in the faculty Bible study.

> **Then Job replied to the LORD: "I know that you can do all things; no purpose of yours can be thwarted."**
>
> —JOB 42:1–2 (NIV)

Our prayers had been for a safe and trustworthy roommate. They were answered with a wink from God as He provided beyond what we could have imagined.

With dorm move-in completed and dinner at a restaurant finished, we toured the campus, looking for each of Kiki's classes. She peered through a window into a small classroom with just a table and twelve chairs and worriedly remarked, "My C. S. Lewis class is so small! What if I don't know enough! There's no way to hide in a classroom that size!" My gut churned as I took in her nervous expression and worried tone. I remembered God's promise from the summer and was determined to trust His placement of her in this small classroom with the conference table and comfortable-looking chairs.

School began and Kiki reported to us that the seasoned professor of her C. S. Lewis class is a follower of Jesus. She finds out this class has a long waiting list and is usually filled with juniors and seniors. The Honors Colloquium class is limited with the intention of creating a small-school experience. She was asked on more than one occasion, "How did you get in there as a freshman?" I felt God wink at me again.

Throughout the fall term, Kiki shared with me all she is learning as this professor leads discussions on the writings of C. S. Lewis in a winsome and instructional way. Kiki began her college career, in part, poring over writings about God and His kingdom—at a state school, no less. It is no small thing that this professor performs his academic rigor in ways that share the truth of Jesus through literature. Monday and Wednesday each week, in an ordinary schedule, students hear extraordinary truths.

Kiki chattered about her affection for her roommate over the next year, and a picture developed of her roommate's loving, Christian home and Godly family. The dad we met, the

> The LORD is a refuge for the oppressed, a stronghold in times of trouble. Those who know your name trust in you, for you, LORD, have never forsaken those who seek you.
>
> —PSALM 9:9–10 (NIV)

university professor, was raising his kids and going to work each day, living his regular life in obedience to God's call. God used it to encourage us through his daughter and by the knowledge of his Jesus-loving presence on campus. We breathed a sigh of relief that lasted the whole school year.

As I look back to the beginning of Kiki's school career and those days in first grade, I remember the fear and doubt I carried when I left her outside of my care, the same feelings I had 12 years later at a college campus. God strategically placed His people in her life to accomplish what He had in store for her. He did it for me too. My trust in Him grew as my children went from grade to grade.

One would think all this trust-building would have made me confident for the next step. It did not. He makes me ready, but my confidence wavers. Although God has brought me along in the process of trusting Him, my fearful mind can't imagine what He will provide through intentionally placed people at university who fear Him. People who demonstrate God's love in their unremarkable day-to-day lives.

Anton Chekhov said, "Any idiot can handle a crisis; it's the day-to-day living that wears you out." And while that might be true, it's also in that day-to-day living that we access God's

> **Therefore, I urge you, brothers and sisters, in view of God's mercy, to offer your bodies as a living sacrifice, holy and pleasing to God—this is your true and proper worship.**
>
> —ROMANS 12:1–2 (NIV)

GOD'S GIFT OF SIGHT
— Linda L. Kruschke —

STANDING ON THE rim of Bryce Canyon in Utah, one is struck by the power and majesty of God. From the rim, it is impossible to see and know the complexity of the canyon's terrain, which is filled with hoodoos (tall, skinny rock formations) and ravines.

In the same way, God seems impossible to know as we stand apart from Him. But just as Bryce becomes more knowable as one descends into the canyon, seeing the chipmunks scampering among the blue spruce and yarrow, God becomes more intimate and loving the more time we spend striving to draw closer to Him.

---

extraordinary power. Daily prayer and scripture, worship, self-examination, communion, community again and again and again. This miraculous monotony is the stuff God uses to infuse us with His power. We benefit from the ordinary in others, and others, in turn, benefit from the ordinary in us, because, let's face it, nothing God does is short of extraordinary.

What will God do with my ordinary? My fear and doubt are still present sometimes. But as I walk in imperfect obedience through each regular day of my life learning to surrender my will and ways to His, I'm expectant that God will spin from it the extraordinary in ways I can't even imagine.

Divine Appointment
Becky Hofstad

On the Monday after Mother's Day, I pulled into the driveway of the farm where I'd grown up, pausing to say another prayer. *Lord, please give me the words.*

I went straight back to Dad's bedroom and sat on the bed opposite his recliner. A warm whisper of a breeze came through the open window. He looked pale, his white hair was disheveled, and his shoulders were hunched over. Dad was now 40 pounds lighter than he'd been at Thanksgiving 6 months ago. We'd all missed the signs that something was wrong.

We'd first heard the words *incurable* and *terminal* less than 3 weeks before. The last round of testing took a toll on him, and he'd made his decision: no treatment. My three siblings and I were raised on this farm; working hard was what we knew best. Doing nothing felt unfamiliar. It felt like failure.

After asking about my daughters, he said, "I was surprised no one fought me," slurring some of his words.

"You're going to a better place," I told him even though he already knew it. "It doesn't make any sense to be miserable here." He reached for the mug of water on the side table and sipped from the straw.

"The Bible says in Revelation that in eternity there will be trees that produce a different crop every month." He smiled and nodded, almost as if envisioning this agricultural wonder.

While we talked, the rest of the farmhouse buzzed with activity. My sister Amanda baked peanut butter cookies while the washing machine ran. My sister Vikki recorded what Dad ate and when. She listed phone calls to make, tasks for each of us to do, and the meals we would eat to keep up our strength. Her highest priority, though, was the schedule for visits. Friends and family wanted to see Dad to say goodbye, but we were cautious about sapping his dwindling strength.

> **We can make our plans, but the LORD determines our steps.**
>
> —PROVERBS 16:9 (NLT)

The next day went mostly according to plan. Dad did a video call with his cousin Bob before shuffling from his recliner in the bedroom to the kitchen table. He leaned on a walker, while Vikki walked backward in front of him to stabilize the walker. I was the caboose of our train, following behind with a rolling office chair to catch him if he fell backward. We were relieved when Dad got seated at the table and could catch his breath. His pastor arrived to outline the funeral service, then talked to Dad alone and served him communion. Before the nurse arrived to set up hospice, Dad was worn out. Vikki and I helped him back to the bedroom using our mobility train. Hospice would put in an order for a wheelchair.

Midafternoon, when Mom came home from her 2-hour shift at the little post office in town, she had an addition to the schedule for the next day "Keith is going to be here tomorrow."

"Mom, tomorrow cousin Bonnie and John are visiting in the morning," Vikki reminded her, "and the afternoon is reserved for the social worker and bath aide from hospice."

The curtness in her voice was protective: there was too much on the schedule.

"He's known your dad a long time," Mom said. "He wants to come."

My thoughts went to Dad's brother Larry, and the call we hoped to sneak in after Bonnie's visit. Larry had Alzheimer's and we'd already bumped him from the schedule the day before to make room for a neighbor who stopped by unexpectedly.

Vikki grabbed her phone and went outside to get better cell reception. She intended to ask Keith to delay his visit, but he was already on the road headed north from Iowa to Minnesota. He'd left immediately after talking with Mom, as though he knew something we didn't.

The next morning, Dad was too weak to use his walker. He rode out to the kitchen in the office chair. He fell asleep a few times at the table during the visit with his cousin and her husband, only eating one bite of rhubarb crisp before they left.

Keith pulled in the driveway as Dad's cousin pulled out. We left Mom and the two 80-year-old men at the kitchen table. They discussed the whirlwind of testing and doctors' visits over the previous weeks. Keith sobbed as he told Dad that he was his best friend in Minnesota.

"Remember the early days when we'd get a group of farmers together to tell them about converting their fields to organic?" he asked Dad. Keith was the fertilizer dealer, and Dad, his client, provided the testimonial. "Some of them thought we were crazy," Keith continued. "That was before organic became trendy. When it was still for fruits and nuts." They both chuckled.

Before Mom left for her afternoon shift, she said, "Your dad has perked up." It was true. Dad was fully engaged in the conversation.

While the men continued to talk, Vikki and I went outside to sit on the deck. Just as I exhaled a deep breath of fresh air, Dad hollered, "Vikki, get my shoes! I want to go out to the fields." I looked at Vikki in disbelief. Dad hadn't been out to the fields in weeks. *What was going on?*

"I asked him how long it had been since he'd been out to his fields," Keith admitted sheepishly when we came inside.

"I can ride in the Bobcat," Dad insisted, his voice clear, strong, and nonnegotiable. The utility vehicle had been Dad's go-to ride out to the fields. Without any further discussion, Vikki ran to park the Bobcat near the end of the ramp leading from the house to the driveway. On her way out the door, she reminded me that the hospice social worker was due in 30 minutes.

> **Show me the right path, O LORD; point out the road for me to follow.**
>
> —PSALM 25:4 (NLT)

I went to look for Dad's shoes. Tapping his hand against the table, he offered suggestions about where they might be.

"Call your mother," he said. My father, the farmer who'd listened to classical music and played racquetball into his 60s, was determined to see the land he had worked for over 40 years.

Vikki found the shoes, and together we managed to get his feet into them. Rolling the office chair to the outside door was easy, but the chair—with Dad in it—wouldn't roll over the lip of the threshold to the deck.

"Let me get another chair," I said to Vikki. "I'll bring it to the other side and then he can pivot into it."

Dad heaved himself up out of the office chair with Vikki standing behind him. We'd forgotten the gait belt the hospice nurse had brought the day before. Vikki guided Dad's shoulder, and he plopped into chair number two. We both stood downhill of the wheeled chair, preventing it from getting out of control as it rolled down the ramp.

Vikki tossed Keith the keys and said, "Good luck! You're driving."

"I don't know how to drive this thing," he confessed, wide-eyed, and slid into the middle of the seat.

Dad stood up. With his tongue out like a small boy to aid in concentration, he leaned his weight on the edge of the seat and grabbed the support bar. Vikki and I helped him lift one foot and then the other into the vehicle. She ran around to take the driver's seat. I readied my phone to take a photo. Dad reached across Keith for the key in the ignition, a crazed look in his eyes that said, "Enough with the delays."

> **Take my yoke upon you. Let me teach you, because I am humble and gentle at heart, and you will find rest for your souls.**
>
> —MATTHEW 11:29 (NLT)

The two octogenarians and my sister took off up the driveway while I sent the photo to my other sister and brother. Then I wondered: *Was this joyride a hospice violation? Was Dad allowed to leave the house?* Withholding what would be his last spin around the dirt roads he'd traveled countless times didn't seem right. Dad also didn't ask for our permission.

The hospice social worker told us later that afternoon that Dad's spin around the farm was "exactly what he should be doing." It didn't hurt him and it brought him joy. It also brought me the peace to let him go. Four days later he passed away on his farm surrounded by his family.

I know God disrupted our schedule that day. He'd prompted Keith to get in his car and drive 6 hours to see his friend who was dying. Yet by our trying to control the situation, Dad had nearly missed the divine appointment.

I pray that I won't forget this lesson of Dad's last days. That I'll practice letting go of the control I think I have. That I won't allow "busy" to distract me. That instead, I will look for the divine appointments God brings into my life.

A Friend for the Write Time

Bettie Boswell

When I submitted my first manuscript for a novel, I discovered I had a lot to learn. I was disappointed, to say the least, that my work wasn't ready for publication. To help expand my skills, I decided to take classes and join groups of fellow writers.

After my failure as a novelist, I turned my interest to working on a story for children. I taught elementary children on a daily basis and thought that experience would give me a better connection with potential readers. I did my research and was excited to discover a secular group of writers for children that met at a library less than a half hour away.

I headed off to my first meeting full of trepidation. Could I write well enough to fit in? Would someone there be knowledgeable enough to teach me? As a Christian writer would I find fellowship with the strangers at the meeting? Would my first attempts at writing for children fail like my novel?

I arrived a little early and cautiously introduced myself. The group was a good size, due in part to several younger people visiting from a college that offered a degree in writing. The local leader, who would later become a teacher for some great workshops I attended, decided to divide the crowd into two groups. We were to take turns sharing a portion of what we were working on and then receive comments that would help our story. I learned this was called a critique session.

We introduced ourselves and began sharing manuscripts. About fifteen minutes into our discussion, a woman who introduced herself as Ann entered our circle. She was late because her husband, who was driving her, had trouble finding the meeting place. When it was her turn, she shared a portion of her middle grade novel for the critique. Her story seemed well-written to me and the others. Later, I shared my work in progress and received some helpful feedback for future drafts, learning new things about the book market in the process.

> **And my God will meet all your needs according to the riches of his glory in Christ Jesus.**
>
> —PHILIPPIANS 4:19 (NIV)

After the critique session finished, the two groups mingled, making friendly connections. As we chatted, Ann revealed she lived in the same town as me. When she mentioned her husband's driving issues, I felt inspired to offer a ride to the next meeting. It felt like a match made in heaven when we discovered she lived less than a mile from my house.

After transporting her to several similar events, we discovered a common desire to write stories reflecting Christian values. I mentioned the Christian romance manuscript that lay gathering dust in my files. Ann said she would be glad to look at my novel; she had gone to several novel-writing workshops in the past and had tips to share. We began trading novel manuscripts and meeting once a month, which was more often than the bigger critique group came together.

As time passed, I learned from Ann's comments on my story. I also took classes about writing for children and adults, which gave me the skills to make helpful suggestions for her writing. Together we built each other up as our writing abilities grew. We went less and less to the secular meetings and continued going over manuscripts with each other monthly. The two of us wanted the freedom to share elements of faith in our stories.

Our individual strengths complemented each other. I might spot a plot hole in her stories, while she found my grammatical errors with ease. We both grew in our ability to improve story, plot, character development, wordplay, setting descriptions, and grammar. God had provided the perfect critique partner for my writing.

> **Therefore encourage one another and build each other up, just as in fact you are doing.**
>
> —1 THESSALONIANS 5:11 (NIV)

God also provided a great friendship. As Ann's husband became more housebound, I stopped by to visit more frequently. We started printing out manuscripts on paper so she could critique while sitting next to her husband in their living room. Those extra visits became pleasant conversations about life in general.

Ann is a prayer warrior who continues to offer petitions for needs in my family and hers. She was always glad to have someone stop in who understood her caregiving situation. She was often in my prayers, too, as she struggled to balance writing and the realities of elder care, until her husband passed.

Together we have cheered each other on when there were successes or mourned together over rejected manuscripts.

> And we know that in all things God works for the good of those who love him, who have been called according to his purpose.
>
> —ROMANS 8:28 (NIV)

She was supportive when I received a novel contract before she had an offer. I encouraged her to keep trying, and she did. Then her time came for that first fiction contract. We are now both published authors with Christian publishers, thanks to a chance meeting at a secular workshop.

God knew what we needed even before we did. You never know when He will provide the perfect connection to improve your life. A kind offer for a ride provided a friend for life. It also opened the door to a learning connection that allowed both of us to achieve long-held dreams of writing for the Christian market. I thank the Lord for His provision.

God is speaking to all of us, all the time. The question is not, to whom does God talk? The question is, who listens?

—Neale Donald Walsch

CHAPTER 3

Listening to God's Voice

"To Do" or "To Be"? 112
    Tara Johnson
God's Many Voices 118
    Linda J. Reeves
Peace in the Storm 125
    Kathryn C. Lang
The God of Placement 131
    Pamela Horton
Transitions 137
    Rachel M. Mathew
The Death of George 143
    Valorie Bridges Fant
I Remembered Your Prayer 149
    Allison Lynn

"To Do" or "To Be"?

Tara Johnson

Milk. Check. Eggs. Check. Bread. Check. Laundry detergent. Check.

I stopped pushing the grocery cart in the crowded store, scanning my list one more time. Only three items left to purchase.

My oldest girl, in all her teenage drama, rolled her eyes. "C'mon, Mom. We're never going to get home if you keep stopping. Why do you need a list anyway? You carry them with you everywhere."

My second daughter snickered from her place at my side. "Because she's getting old."

The two jokesters giggled as I offered a mock frown of indignation. "Old, huh? I guess I'm too old to remember to buy you the Oreos you want."

The girls offered their best angelic "I'm sorry" smiles as we wove our way through crying toddlers, cranky fathers, and frazzled mothers. The shopping cart rattled noisily. A monotone voice dripped from the overhead speakers.

"Carla, register five, please." How could anyone concentrate in all the chaos?

My oldest snagged the list from my hand and scanned the remaining items. "Why do you use checklists anyway? You have them plastered all over the house."

I pushed the cart past the meat section. "Honestly? I have so much crammed in my brain, I'm afraid I'm going to forget something. Plus, when I cross it off, it makes me feel like I've accomplished a monumental task." I shrugged. "Silly, I know. Or maybe it gives me the illusion of control. Like I'm keeping all the spinning plates up and moving."

Pursing her lips, my teen handed back the slip of paper. "I get that. But I wonder if you would freak out if the lists ever got lost or thrown away."

I laughed. "I would probably panic a little."

My second daughter squeezed my hand and looked up into my face, her expression sweet. "Even if you were disorganized, or lost your to-do lists, you'd still be a great mom."

> For I have given you an example, that you also should do just as I have done to you.
>
> —JOHN 13:15 (ESV)

As we left the crowded store that day, I reflected on my kids' comments. To-do lists are helpful but they aren't what make a good mother, father, friend, sister, teacher, or anything else. Plowing through chores doesn't mean I have good character, just like counting steps on a Fitbit during vacation doesn't ensure an enjoyable trip.

I don't just want to *do* more . . . I want to *be* more. Maybe that's why each day feels like I'm scraping my way through concrete. It shouldn't be about cramming more into jam-packed schedules. It should be about pursuing Jesus.

After arriving home and tucking away the groceries, I sat down with a pad of paper and a pencil to make a new list—a running compilation of who I wanted to be. In a matter of minutes, I had run out of room on the page.

To Be:
Compassionate
Loving
Kind
Less prideful
Less stubborn
Teachable
Look at people through God's eyes
Wise
Slow to speak
Serene
Joyful
Encouraging
Prayerful
Seeker of God's heart . . .

The longer I gripped my pencil, the more I realized I was circling around one person, one focal point. All these character traits and more were compressed and displayed in the person of Christ. Scanning the list, it became clear: I want to be like Jesus.

The previous week, our pastor had preached on 1 John 2:6 (NASB1995), and it rolled through my brain as I stared at the pencil marks: "The one who says he abides in Him ought himself to walk in the same manner as He walked."

So to be like Jesus, I just need to walk like Jesus. Got it. Check that off the list.

If only it were that easy.

That's kind of a tall order, you know? It's like saying to be a great basketball player, play like Michael Jordan. To be pretty, look like Cindy Crawford. It seems unattainable. Some days, it's downright impossible.

Before I crumpled the overwhelming list in my hand, I took a deep breath. The Lord knows I'm not perfect, and He knows I have messed up and will continue to mess up. That's why He sent His Son.

> Love is patient, love is kind. It does not envy, it does not boast, it is not proud. It does not dishonor others, it is not self-seeking, it is not easily angered, it keeps no record of wrongs. Love does not delight in evil but rejoices with the truth.
>
> —1 CORINTHIANS 13:4–5 (NIV)

The idea isn't to be sinless—it's to strive to be like Him. To please Him. To know His heart. To let Him mold me into the image of His Son.

So like any good, organized girl does, I made yet another checklist.

How Did Jesus Walk?

1. *His prayer time with God was long and a priority.*
2. *He sought out the broken, rejected, abused, mistreated, and social outcasts.*
3. *His concern was doing God's will, and only God's will.*
4. *He battled temptation with scripture.*
5. *He touched the untouchables.*

6. *He made people mad.*
7. *He spoke the truth.*
8. *He was a God pleaser, not a people pleaser.*
9. *He wasn't consumed with material wealth.*
10. *He did not chastise the broken for being broken. He offered them Living Water instead.*
11. *He served those He knew would betray and abandon Him.*
12. *He wept for people who rejected Him.*
13. *He forgave.*
14. *He offered compassion.*
15. *He loved people, even when they were messy.*

This list barely scratches the surface, but it's a start. I may never be all I should be, but with His help, I can strive to respond like Jesus, to show forgiveness like Jesus, to extend a hand like Jesus and love like He does.

Despite my affinity for meddlesome to-do lists, I think they are overrated. Our culture is so consumed with "do more," schedule-juggling, organizing, managing, and rearranging that we've lost sight of something quite important. I think we've got the whole cram-more-into-your-day-and-wonder-why-we-need-caffeine-and-stress-management-to-keep-up thing down.

> **Set your minds on things that are above, not on earthly things.**
>
> —COLOSSIANS 3:2 (NIV)

No. Better organization isn't the problem. What we choose to tackle in a day has less to do with an agenda and more about what our priorities are. In other words, *to do* is not nearly as important as *to be*.

There's an old story that claims when Michelangelo revealed his masterpiece statue of David, a man asked him, "However did you create such a breathtaking work out of nothing more than a block of lifeless marble?"

Michelangelo replied, "It is not difficult. A person need only chip away the parts that do not resemble David."

That's what God wants to do with us—chip away the hard stuff in our hearts and lives until we look like His Son.

A good way to start? Drop the to-do lists and focus on how to be like Christ. When we shift our focus on *to be*, our to-do list rewrites itself.

And isn't that a relief? No more lists.

Check.

God's Many Voices
Linda J. Reeves

God speaks to me through the voices and expressions of other people, often strangers. He enlightens me with thoughtful, dramatic, warm, and funny experiences. On occasion, He has literally spoken to me—not out loud, but loudly. An interruption to my own thoughts. Like this one, each word enunciated: *Put your seat belt on.*

It's only a block and a half, I thought. Yet trusting Him, I complied. Moments later, I was hit hard by the driver behind me who ignored the red light. No one was injured.

From an early age, I've known God's will through instinct and observation, both of which help me know when He's speaking to me. I listen carefully and then gratefully follow His guidance. The one time I didn't was another of those rare moments when I actually heard His voice. What He asked of me would have meant giving up long-anticipated plans that started in high school when I heard a missionary speak of his work in Africa. Inspired, I sought advice from my pastor.

"I think God might be calling me to serve Him," I said. "What do I do now?"

"Seminary," he replied. "You should go to seminary."

It wasn't the answer I expected, but I took it seriously. Go to college, then seminary. The only problem, as I would learn later, was that I didn't ask God what I should do.

Before my last year of college, I visited the seminary only 5 hours away. Excited, I started walking through the main building and saw the sign for Admissions. Right away, I felt an uneasiness that grew as I walked past other offices. I knew God was speaking to me as He often does—using my surroundings to help me understand His message. This time He was saying, *This is not for you.*

Driving home, I cried, feeling devastated and confused. I pulled over and looked toward the setting sun as though it were the face of God. Through tears, I prayed, "What do You *want* me to do?"

Two words, spoken insistently, pushed aside my thoughts: *Missionary journeyman.*

Stunned, I stopped crying and said in frustration, "I don't even know what that means." Instantly I recalled meeting someone a long time before who'd been to Japan as a "journeyman."

"Wait a minute," I said. "I don't want to leave the country."

There ended the discussion.

I soon learned the Missionary Journeyman program was for young adults in the Baptist faith to serve 2 years in international missions. I knew God wanted me to apply, but I still hoped there might be room for negotiation. The process was extensive and, despite God's clarity, I was certain I would not be selected.

Months later, I received a letter inviting me to a screening conference. Among other events, we were to meet individually with a mission representative. At some point, my evaluator introduced himself and led me to an interview room.

"I'm supposed to ask you questions," he said with a smile, "but let me start by saying you will be very happy in Argentina."

I was astounded. We'd been encouraged to choose assignments in three countries and, if appointed, we were guaranteed one of them.

"But I didn't choose Argentina," I told him.

"You'll fit in really well," he continued.

"I don't know anything about Argentina."

"This assignment is perfect for you," he assured me, "and I know because I was a missionary there."

"I've studied Spanish for years," I pressed, "and I could work in Peru or Ecuador . . ."

"That'll help you with Castellano, the language they speak in Argentina. It's actually Spanish mixed with Italian and other influences. You won't have any trouble!"

I gave up. For the rest of the interview, he talked about life in Buenos Aires—the clothes, the foods, the customs, and most of all the people.

"You'll love them," he said wistfully, "and they will love you."

It was no surprise when a few weeks later I received a letter informing me I'd been accepted into the program and assigned to Argentina.

> **The heavens declare the glory of God; the skies proclaim the work of his hands. They have no speech, they use no words; no sound is heard from them. Yet their voice goes out into all the earth, their words to the ends of the world.**
>
> —PSALM 19:1, 3–4 (NIV)

After graduation, 8 weeks of training began with an emphasis on adapting to a new culture. At one point, someone quietly asked, "How do I know if this is God's will for me?"

Our instructor answered, "You will have a sense of rightness that will continue to grow."

Yes, I thought, *or sometimes God just tells you.*

In the last week of training, I received calls from three people who were involved in missions but not directly with our training. They each wanted to meet with me briefly to discuss my appointment to Argentina. Such consultations were not in our schedule, so I was intrigued.

The first visitor was a missionary who'd spent most of her life in Argentina.

"Get to know the Argentines. Some journeymen choose English-speaking churches and never fully experience the culture. Join a Spanish-speaking church and you'll know the blessing of belonging."

The second visitor was a young woman who introduced herself as a missionary kid (MK).

"Don't ignore the MKs. Their parents have a calling, but some of the children think it's not fair to them. They feel like outsiders, isolated and forgotten. They need for you to see them, listen to them, and love them."

And the third visitor was a man who had worked with several international missions.

"Spend time with the missionaries. They are truly extraordinary people. Journeymen often become immersed in their own assignments and never take time to visit missionaries in other parts of the country."

God was clearly speaking to me, but it was hard to keep up!

Before long, I was on the 5,000-mile flight to Buenos Aires. My assignment on weekdays would be to help with administrative services for the 90 missionaries in the country. From the moment I stepped off the plane, I felt excitement about this new experience.

> For God does speak—now one way, now another—though no one perceives it. In a dream, in a vision of the night, when deep sleep falls on people as they slumber in their beds.
>
> —JOB 33:14–15 (NIV)

Get to know the Argentines. That first Sunday, a missionary family took me to a small church in the neighborhood. Everything was in Spanish, and I loved singing the hymns. When the service ended, three older teenagers came running over and introduced themselves.

"Would you like to sing with our group?" one of them asked.

"What?"

They explained they wrote gospel songs and performed them at parks and special events.

"I'm just an alto," I said with a questioning look.

"We know! We heard you singing harmony, and that's what we need!"

I had lunch with their family, and soon I was rehearsing with the group. Being part of their lives and joining the church helped me assimilate quickly. I learned Castellano and came to know, as promised, the blessing of belonging.

Don't ignore the MKs. Then came the semi-annual mission meeting, when we all enjoyed a week of fellowship and recreation. As I arrived, a man ran up to me and said, "We have a special job for you!"

He told me about three 10-year-old boys who were too rowdy at times.

"We were hoping you could work with them for part of the day."

"Every day?"

He nodded and picked up my guitar to carry it into the room where we were gathering. As he set it down, I remembered how a 10-year-old boy had taught me the first three chords I ever learned. I could do at least that much!

Whether you turn to the right or to the left, your ears will hear a voice behind you, saying, "This is the way; walk in it."

—ISAIAH 30:21 (NIV)

I asked the boys if they knew how to play guitar. None of them did, but they all wanted to learn. So I borrowed a few instruments for class and taught them those three basic chords—G, C, and D. It took time to master the chords, and the boys bravely worked past their sore fingertips. Then we added some familiar songs and pretended we were on stage. Early on, word spread and other MKs viewed me as a friend and, down the line, a confidant.

Spend time with the missionaries. That directive proved challenging because of distance and scheduling. Still, I'd go whenever I was invited to visit them on weekends. I participated in their church events and spent time with their families.

Some of the missionaries worked in cities, some in villages. Others built small churches in isolated and rugged areas where there were no other places of worship. In one of those churches, I met an elderly man who rode a train 2 hours each way to attend services. In awe, I asked him why.

He smiled and said, "To hear the Bible read aloud and pray with people who love God."

No, it wasn't hard to see the missionaries as extraordinary.

After 2 incredible years, my assignment ended and I had to return to the States. At the airport, three small groups came to say goodbye—Argentines, MKs, and missionaries. Gradually, we moved into one big circle of laughter and tears. Looking around at their beautiful faces, I saw the love and acceptance they had given me and the rich friendships I could have missed had I not followed God's guidance.

Although I had listened to His voice, telling me exactly what He wanted me to do, I'd responded with hesitation and doubt. Step by step, God taught me a deeper level of trust that relies on strong faith and mutual respect. It's simple. I trust Him to lead, and He trusts me to follow. It is then when we both enjoy the blessings that come.

Peace in the Storm
Kathryn C. Lang

The unexpected silence was deafening without the usual hum of electricity and electronics. The only sounds were the underbrush crunching with the footsteps of hidden creatures, the tension-spiked voices of my family, and my pounding heartbeat.

Most people will agree that the world changed in March of 2020. On Easter night, April 12, of that same year, a tornado landed on our home, and it didn't even leave behind any ruby slippers. That's when my world really changed.

We were alive and unhurt, but the tornado that had just passed over us left a wake of destruction. We had huddled in the hall closet, my youngest son (14 at the time) shoved in the back, followed by me, then my 79-year-old dad hovering over me, and finally my husband, who was standing guard between all of us and the storm.

Lightning flashes provided the only visual clues of the damage, but the fact I could see the bare mountainside from the interior closet told me all I needed to know. We climbed out of the rubble to make our way to safety. The dozens of old-growth hardwood trees around our house had toppled like dominoes, forcing us to navigate a maze in the dark.

"Thank You, God, for keeping us all safe." I don't know if I said the words out loud. I do know I clung to them as I tried to control the sobs wracking my heart. I took deep breaths to try to regain control. How do you hold on to control when there is a literal hole ripped through your life? Everyone was unharmed, including our pets. The two dogs, and the cat that was certain he was a dog, showed up as we started out to safety. It was the glint of hope in the depth of the darkness.

We spent the next 7 weeks corralled in a hotel because we were unable to find a rental in our community. The glamour of hotel living featured on television shows is a lie, especially when you are locked in quarantine.

> **Be still and know that I am God.**
>
> —PSALM 46:10 (NIV)

My husband and I decided early on to make all our decisions from a place of peace, not from a place of fear—and to rely on God.

"God. I've never asked for anything this specific, but You say to ask. I have never lived on the lake, and it would be nice to do that at least once." My husband offered the prayer when we had drained all our resources and connections, trying to find a place to call home until our house could be repaired.

My husband noticed the owner of the hotel in the lobby that morning and told him our situation. That afternoon, someone walked into his real estate office to list a rental house he owned.

"Would you consider renting it out instead?" my husband asked. The next morning we were signing a lease for a house, just across the street from the lake. The owners, who used this house as a vacation property, told us we could stay as long as we needed. We expected to stay 6 months since the insurance policy told us we would be compensated.

We settled in, made new friends, and explored the lakefront area. My husband and I spent most mornings praying on the front porch as we watched the sunrise over the lake. We walked together around the lake. My dad, who lived with us after my mom passed, would join us in the evening for the sunset—his favorite time of day. We were enjoying where we were on the way to where we were going.

God led our way, and we leaned on the peace that passes all understanding. I landed two unexpected freelancing jobs doing what I love: writing encouragement articles for one company and planning events for another. When one of our two farm dogs passed away unexpectedly, we had the time and the space to bring her brother inside. He had never lived inside, but he walked right into the crate we had purchased for him and went to sleep. Just like that, he went from farm dog to indoor dog.

Everything was going the way it was supposed to go until it wasn't.

Turns out, people don't always hold to their promises. The owner of our temporary home sold it, and the new owner wanted to move in. Since we were on a month-to-month rental, we had to pack and go. Again, God led us to a place to meet our needs—a space for my dad, room to spread out and work since both of my jobs were remote from home, and acceptance of our dog.

And then insurance stopped paying. Between the denials and the delays, what had been paid wasn't enough to fix our home. Now, our insurance company wouldn't pay to keep us in a rental. But the additional jobs I had picked up covered the rent.

Until the owner of this space decided he wanted to use it.

A couple of weeks before we had to move, my husband reached out to another owner in the complex where we were staying. This space was bigger than we'd rented before, but more important than space was a flexible rent option because we didn't know how long the insurance would drag out the payment of our policy.

The owner agreed to our request.

Just like that, we were in a better position than we had been. We could move all the property we had managed to salvage from the tornado into the new space. It almost felt like home.

> **The LORD will fight for you; you need only be still.**
>
> —EXODUS 14:14 (NIV)

The emotional tornado we had been living through seemed to lose its energy. Until the day my husband got notice that his job would not be continuing in the upcoming year. Shortly after that, my two freelance jobs ended. We were left without any income, without a home, and with an insurance policy that wouldn't pay.

It's hard to have peace when the storm is that loud. The only thing I knew to do was to believe in the promises I had been reading in Scripture. So I made a list of those promises. Then I made a list of all the good things coming from this storm: We lived on the lake. We made new friends. I had the chance to plan and implement my first big-name concert. My husband and I were praying together. I was growing bolder in praying openly for others.

Despite the circumstances, peace prevailed.

Too often, just when I think I have it all together, something major happens. This time, it was my dad. We started noticing little things about his memory and his attitude. After a major surgery to remove a cancerous spot on his kidney, my dad got worse. We had to move him to an assisted living facility, and then 2 short months later, he was gone.

Darkness crashed around me again. I cupped the tiny glint of hope that remained protectively in my hands. "I believe; help my unbelief" (Mark 9:24, ESV). I knew the words in the Bible, but I wasn't believing the way I knew I should. All I could do was keep repeating the words and pray that the dawn would finally break. A song that kept coming up on my streaming service reminded me something was about to break. I didn't know it would be me.

Three months later, the insurance company dealt the final blow. We were told they didn't have to honor their policy and that they had paid us all they would pay. We were on our own.

> **Do not be anxious about anything, but in every situation, by prayer and petition, with thanksgiving, present your requests to God.**
>
> —PHILIPPIANS 4:6 (NIV)

The tiny glint of hope flickered out. I broke. I was mad at the system. I was mad at people. I was especially mad at God. I thought I had gone all in for God and with God. Nothing had worked out the way I had expected.

How could I keep going when everything was falling around me? How could I be an encouragement to others when hope didn't reside in my heart? How could I believe when I was covered with unbelief?

I was driving, so I could do nothing except sulk and plan for what I would do when I got home. I would quit my podcast. I would quit my blog. I would quit my encouragement groups. I would just give in to the world's way and go along to get along. Nothing else had worked for me.

My husband texted our two older sons, who were away at college, with the latest news. The oldest was the first to reply.

"God's got this."

Three words.

I would never have believed that three words shared in a text would make such an impact, but they were the perfect eye in the middle of my storm. My son had seen my walk and my faith through his growing-up years, and he was pouring it back onto me and into me.

Peace. Three words severed the darkness and planted a new glint of hope in my heart.

Peace gave me the strength to stand and the wisdom to begin to help my unbelief.

Have peace. Be still. God's got this.

The God of Placement
Pamela Horton

I grew up an army brat, and when I was a child, my family attended Protestant services on the army base where we were stationed. We were regulars, until my dad returned from Vietnam. After that, we didn't go to church anymore. I never questioned it. I did ask to set up a candlelight service in the living room each Christmas Eve, where I read Luke 2. I felt it was important to remember the birth of Christ.

After high school, I married the first person who asked me. We were married by my grandfather, who was a minister. Our son was baptized as an infant because that's what you do. However, we never attended a church service or acknowledged God's existence. My first marriage was not the happy, peaceful relationship I longed for, and eventually we divorced.

In 1987, I met Jim at his sister's wedding. I had not been looking for a relationship, and I turned him down when he asked me out. But he pursued me, not in a scary way, but in a kind, sweet manner that allowed me to feel cherished. He was everything my first husband was not. Jim and I were married in March of 1988 and moved to Syracuse, New York, shortly after for his job.

We moved often as we progressed in our marriage, parenthood, and careers. Having moved often as a child, these times weren't stressful for me—they were simply a part of life. Looking back on my adult life moves, I can see God's hand in each one through the people He placed in our path. That is why I refer to Him as the God of Placement.

Because we were busy in a new marriage and not church-goers at the time, it took the birth of our son to bring church back to mind. Jim had grown up Catholic and fallen away from church when he went to college. When our son was born, Jim wanted him baptized in the Catholic church. We found a wonderful church and became very involved. Jim was a Minister of the Word, and I taught First Communion classes. We enjoyed the fellowship and realized how much we missed God. We felt like we had come home, much like the prodigal son. We knew God had brought us together and to this church to bring us back to Him. However, in 1992, Jim had a better business opportunity, and we moved to Middletown, New York, a few hours south of Syracuse.

> A man's heart plans his way, but the LORD directs his steps.
>
> —PROVERBS 16:9 (NKJV)

We struggled to find a church that we liked. Life got busy, and we fell away again. However, Jim's boss was a strong Christian man who stretched Jim's thinking. We couldn't see it then, but God was working, planting seeds that would grow. Then we moved to Connecticut but were only there 1 year when the company was sold. Jim had to find a new job. We later learned that God allows certain things as growth opportunities.

In 1996, we transferred to Pennsylvania and found a Catholic church to attend, but it wasn't the same as the one we loved in Syracuse. We were back in church but were basically doing rote religion. We didn't find joy in attendance or get involved in serving. Getting our boys to go was a challenge, and our oldest refused confirmation and walked away from the church. Four years later Jim had another job change. This was the longest we had lived anywhere, and while we loved our friends, we looked forward to finding a new church where we could fit in.

In 2001, we moved to Ashburn, Virginia. Our oldest son had moved to Florida. Our younger son made friends with a pastor's son, so we started going to their small gatherings. It was the first time I heard people speak out in service. I was uncomfortable with that, and I remember praying, "Please don't let me say anything." Consequently, we rarely attended church. Soon, Jim was making another career move. Yet it was not devastating for us, as we still had not found a church community where we felt God's joy.

It was our move to Blue Ridge, Virginia, where we recognized God was with us and our lives began to change. In this neighborhood were twin boys the same age as our son. They invited him to a Super Bowl party at church, just down the street. Soon, he started asking to go to church with the neighbors. We were amazed. We used to drag our boys to church, and now he was asking to go! Jim and I decided we better go check out this place. It was a Baptist church, and we had no experience with that denomination.

This was a church of about 1,500 people. The pastor asked our names and welcomed us. We sat in the back and kept to ourselves, but were interested enough to return the following week. When the pastor welcomed us by name, I was ready to call this our new church. Everyone brought their Bible to church, so we had to buy Bibles. This was all new to Jim. He had never read the Bible before. I went to a Christian bookstore and asked for guidance purchasing a Bible. I was shown an entire wall of Bibles. I was overwhelmed with the options. I said, "I just want The Bible," and they were stumped. I added, "The original Bible." I walked out with a small leather-bound King James Version with no study notes for $5. It was perfect and is now falling apart from use.

One day we noticed a very tall man from the church praise team walking down the street with his wife. We introduced ourselves, and they have become lifelong friends. They invited us to a Bible study at their home. We attended that weekly meeting for 8 years. Our knowledge, understanding, and faith grew by leaps and bounds. We were challenged to read through the entire Bible in a year. Jim continues this practice to this day, 20 years later. We became very involved with serving in the church and came to realize that faith is not about religion but about a relationship.

> **For I know the thoughts that I think toward you, says the LORD, thoughts of peace and not of evil, to give you a future and a hope.**
>
> —JEREMIAH 29:11 (NKJV)

I was shocked when Jim announced he wanted to be baptized. He truly wanted to show his new faith to the world. We were baptized on Jim's birthday in 2004. We both felt like we'd finally found a place and a church we could call home. We had been in Blue Ridge for 8 years when God called us to move again. I questioned His purpose. We loved our friends and our church. Why was He moving us? We would later discover His reason in His time.

This was the hardest move I'd ever had to make. We had put down roots in Blue Ridge. Our oldest son was there, with our two grandchildren. My family was together again, and we had to leave them. Many tears were shed. Thankfully, we were only going to be 4 hours away in North Carolina.

Once we settled in, the search for a church began quickly. We knew we wanted to be in a church like the one we had just left. We visited 20 churches when I heard about a large, non-denominational church and suggested we visit. Jim was skeptical, but when he heard the praise team, he was sold. His requirements were few: great worship music and a biblically based, powerful message. This church checked those boxes. We were home.

> **For it is God who works in you both to will and to do for His good pleasure.**
>
> —PHILIPPIANS 2:13 (NKJV)

Two years later, Jim was feeling burned out from corporate life when a job opened at church. The person doing the interviewing oversaw the ministry where Jim volunteered, and he got the job! The relief he felt leaving corporate and working for a church let us know this was the reason we were in North Carolina. It is at this church where we've been able to share our story, our knowledge, and our faith with others. It's a blessing to help others grow in their faith, as we were helped by others. However, after 10 years with the church, Jim is retiring, and we are moving again.

As we looked toward this new move, we've talked about the moves we have made, the people who were put in our path, and those paths we have walked with others. We can see God's wisdom in it all. He took us to places where we grew in His

Word and left us in places with weeds for only a short time. We wonder who God has planned for us to meet in our new location and what our journey will look like. Looking back, we recognize that God was with us all along and set us in the places that would most benefit our coming to know Him more. God is truly the God of Placement.

Transitions
Rachel M. Mathew

Getting laid off is an emotional experience, even for a professional counselor who has lots of coping tools! The decision-making board of the church I worked for had decided to close its onsite counseling center for the summer. I had been given just 2 weeks to make arrangements for my clients. I was furious! It made no sense, but I had not been consulted and had no recourse. There went my summer income!

After a few days of a very bad attitude and lots of complaining to my husband, I decided I'd had enough. I was going to retire. One by one I made provisions for the needs of the clients, and then I started discharging the few clients I saw at another church. Soon the day came for my very last appointment with my last client.

Before that appointment I'd completed a couple of chores at home. Out on our sunny Florida lanai I worked with one hand, moving plants from the plant stand to the table, dusting the stand, and then moving them back again. The other hand was holding my phone to my ear. I was talking to one of my very favorite people, a friend who was always an absolute delight. I was tickled to have this short time talking with her even though I soon had to leave for work. Linda and I had connected over a deep love of Jesus, Israel, and sheep, in that order. We were talking about all three of these.

Linda kept sheep at her small farm and I loved to visit there and watch them. I was excited to hear she was preparing to lead a group of parishioners from her church on a tour of Israel. She had been there many more times than my two trips; how I wished I could go again, particularly with her!

I told Linda I would soon be heading out to my last counseling appointment and then would be officially retired. Right about that time I clearly heard a word in my mind. The word was *transitions*. It stopped me in my tracks.

"Linda! I just heard a word! I think it was from the Lord!"

Linda and I both believe that God communicates directly to His children even though neither of us had often experienced it. The two of us got to work discussing what the word might mean. All I came up with was that I was transitioning from my career to retirement. Another possibility was that Linda was transitioning from shepherding sheep to shepherding people, a reference to her upcoming tour of Israel.

Later as I was styling my hair and getting ready for work, I talked to God. "Transitions. What does that mean, Lord?" I really did not know.

My last appointment was held in a room graciously provided for my use in a local church. The appointment went well—the client no longer needed counseling, and I felt confident releasing her from my care. After we said goodbye I took

> The LORD says, "I will guide you along the best pathway for your life. I will advise you and watch over you."
>
> —PSALM 32:8 (NLT)

a deep breath and headed to the pastor's office, ready to turn in the key and fill him in on the culmination of the ministry.

Our pastor was a wonderful young man and felt like one of my sons. As I handed him the key I couldn't help but notice the serious expression on his face. He asked where he could refer his parishioners now that I was retired. I told him about a couple of Christian counselors I knew and also about a new secular program in our local hospital. The management at the facility was hoping some local therapists would fill in for existing staff a few hours a month.

Although I was glad for the services they provided, I quickly concluded that I would not want to work there. My reasons were rather shallow. When we toured the facility there were no windows on the unit and everything looked bland and institutional. I am very visually oriented and prefer warm, pleasant surroundings. Truthfully, though, the bigger reason was that I was afraid to work there.

It was a bittersweet ending to my career when I left the pastor's office. Although I knew I would definitely see my pastor friend again, I felt sorry for him and so many others who wished there were more Christian counselors available in our small rural county.

When I got home I went right to my computer to type up a list of the places I'd recommended with contact information for the pastor's convenience. I came to the hospital program—Transitions Behavioral Health. All at once it hit me! *Transitions* was the word the Lord spoke to me earlier in the morning. Could it be He was referring to this program when He said that word earlier? Did that mean He wanted me to work there?

My hand flew to my mouth. "Oh no! Oh no, oh no!" I gasped. I was blown away. It was not the kind of place I wanted to work. I had worked in Christian ministries all of my twenty-plus years in the profession except for a very short stint in community mental health. This would be a strictly secular environment. I had never done much group counseling either. Nearly the whole program at Transitions revolved around back-to-back group sessions. Because it was a program offered by our local hospital, there was an option for partial hospitalization as well as intensive outpatient counseling.

> **Whether you turn to the right or to the left, your ears will hear a voice behind you, saying, "This is the way; walk in it."**
>
> —ISAIAH 30:21 (NIV)

I thought about what I learned at the open house, how the coordinator of the program had appealed for part-time help from professional counselors. I wondered whether they had found the help they needed. There had been a lot of counselors in attendance that day, and I hoped some of them had stepped in to help. Me? I was reluctant to start a new job.

Even though I wasn't interested, I felt the nudge from God. So I looked at the job openings on the hospital website and saw a position for a per diem therapist. I couldn't shake the urge I felt to at least check it out.

I had great respect for the medical director of the program. He had tried unsuccessfully in the past to get such a program started. At last one was up and running. I wanted it to succeed. I had been praying for more mental health services for our county ever since I'd arrived in Florida after my husband's retirement. How could I refuse to be an answer to my own prayers? I took a deep breath and sent his office an email inquiring if the position had been filled.

Soon, I was sitting in one of those bland windowless rooms at a table with the program coordinator and the psychiatric nurse from the program. Between them they had been providing all the services 5 days a week since the program started in March. They handled administrative duties, referrals, intakes, and discharges in addition to all the group sessions and individual therapy. It was now September and the coordinator was unwell. She was coughing and looked extremely fatigued. I learned later that she had the nurse sit in to help with the interview because she was so exhausted she wasn't sure she could evaluate me properly.

> **Here I am! I stand at the door and knock. If anyone hears my voice and opens the door, I will come in. I will eat with that person, and they will eat with me.**
>
> —REVELATION 3:20 (NIRV)

I also found out that the very existence of the program depended on having another master's level licensed mental health professional available. The doors could not be open, nor insurance billed, unless there was such personnel on-site all the hours the program was in operation. The sick young woman, who would become my boss, had not been able to take a day off in 9 months to attend to her own health. I'm sure that is why in spite of my lack of experience in the inpatient setting and with groups, I got a job offer shortly after. Needless to say, when I accepted she was relieved to have me onboard.

GOD'S GIFT OF TOUCH
— Eryn Lynum —

TO TRAP ITS prey, a Venus flytrap utilizes touch receptors called mechanoreceptors. An insect's slight touch or pressure triggers these receptors and creates an electrical signal that shuts the leafy trap. Human skin has mechanoreceptors, too, and God's design allows for us to feel the slightest pressure or sensation, giving us a wealth of information about the world around us. Like other senses, touch can be strengthened and heightened by turning off other sensory inputs, such as closing one's eyes or using noise-canceling headphones. Similarly, we can train ourselves to become more sensitive to God's Holy Spirit, developing a deeper awareness of His gentle pressure on our lives through solitude, silence, and prayer.

That one word, *transitions*, led me to the most challenging job of my career. My friend, Linda, was a great prayer support for me. But that one word from the Lord was my bedrock throughout the experience. It gave me confidence that I was in God's hands and doing His will even though I was stretched way out of my comfort zone.

My goal had been to obey God and to help ensure that the program could continue. I am happy to say the goal was met. After a year and a half, another full-time therapist was hired and I left the program. The Lord did not release me from being a counselor though. As a matter of fact, I still am!

The Death of George

Valorie Bridges Fant

Throughout the early years of my life, the concept of spending time in church was foreign to my family; our interests lay elsewhere. On most weekends, when my parents weren't hosting a lively group of drunken friends at our house, they spent their time on the Corner. The Corner was infamous for its dilapidated bars and shady liquor stores. On any given night, it was likely that someone would be shot or stabbed, making violence commonplace in our small Midwestern town. The scent of stale cigars and fermented whiskey hung in the air like ominous clouds. Creepy old men dressed in wrinkled suits would shout things like, "Hey, girl! Come back here!" whenever I walked past. These childhood memories are indelibly marked in my mind.

However, in the autumn of 1976, my life took a completely unexpected turn after I had a life-changing encounter with God. While taking quiet walks through the woods behind my house, I began to question the meaning of life. *What is life, and where did I come from? What is death, and why am I afraid to die?* I struggled to believe that people were born into this complex world, only to exist for a moment and then die. There had to be a deeper purpose to life. Unbeknownst to me, God was guiding my path. Eventually, He guided me to His Word. I started reading the Bible with an insatiable hunger. Day after day, as I received revelations, I would eagerly share my newfound wisdom with my parents.

One afternoon, as I was reading the Bible, I stumbled upon a verse that completely amazed me. I rushed downstairs to the kitchen, finding my mother washing dishes and my father, George, eating lunch at the table.

"Mama, Mama, guess what Jesus said?" I blurted out. They both turned and stared at me. "Jesus said, if I have the faith of a mustard seed, I can move mountains!"

Giddy with joy, I assumed they would feel the same. However, the reaction I received was not one of excitement. Immediately, a grim expression appeared on Daddy's face. He had a mysterious look in his eyes as he glared at me.

With a disturbingly calm voice, he said, "Val, you're crazy. You're sitting over there looking crazy."

"No, Daddy, this is what Jesus said!" I explained.

My father got up from his chair and slowly walked across the room. He stood over me, much like a giant grizzly bear. Just inches away from my face, he angrily cursed at me. I felt the heat of his breath and caught the scent of his midday meal.

Tears poured from my eyes. I ran upstairs to my closet, recalling a verse I had read: "But you, when you pray, go into

> **I have been crucified with Christ and I no longer live, but Christ lives in me. The life I now live in the body, I live by faith in the Son of God, who loved me and gave himself for me.**
>
> —GALATIANS 2:20 (NIV)

your room, and when you have shut your door, pray to your Father who is in the secret place; and your Father who sees in secret will reward you openly" (Matthew 6:6, NKJV). So, with my face pressed against my clothing, I prayed, "Dear God, please open Daddy's eyes and save him from his sin!"

Two weeks later, while my father sat eating his afternoon lunch, he experienced pain in his chest. My mother rushed him to the local hospital. In less than an hour, they transported him to St. Joseph Mercy Hospital in Ann Arbor, one of the most prestigious hospitals in Michigan. Ann Arbor was only an hour's drive away, so it was even more concerning when I found out Daddy had been medevaced.

When my family and I arrived at the hospital, we anxiously awaited news of my father's condition. After a while, a doctor with a youthful appearance came into the waiting room. He looked barely older than me, which raised my anxiety about his ability to care for my father.

"Mrs. Bridges, your husband has pneumonia," he sympathetically said. "We need to insert a tube into his chest to drain the fluid from his lungs." Upon hearing the doctor's words, fear took hold of my heart.

That evening, they performed the operation, and we cautiously believed it would go according to plan. When the doctor returned, he reported that the implanted tube was too small and they'd have to perform another procedure the next day. In my 19 years of life, I had never felt so helpless. My older sister cradled my hand, silently reassuring me not to worry, but her face betrayed her fear.

In the midst of it all, I whispered prayers to God, desperately hoping He would hear me—begging Him to hear my plea! Before we left the hospital, Mama leaned over and gently kissed

Daddy on his forehead. Tears filled my eyes as I pushed away the thought of never seeing him alive again.

I was so afraid when Mama drove us home that night. Making things even worse, I remembered a nightmarish dream I'd had months earlier. In the dream, I saw myself entering an empty church through two large doors with stained glass windows. Walking just ahead of me was Grandma Vinnie, Daddy's mother. In our family, Grandma Vinnie stood out as a strong, spirited woman with unwavering faith in God. Gently cradled in my arms was a bowl of banana pudding, Daddy's favorite dessert.

> **For nothing is secret that will not be revealed, nor anything hidden that will not be known and come to light.**
>
> —LUKE 8:17 (NKJV)

As we walked down a deep red carpet, I saw two stark white coffins illuminated by the sun's bright light. One was large, and the other was much smaller. We stopped once we reached the coffins. When I peered into the spacious, silk-lined box, Daddy was lying there. Inside the other was my little brother, Lance. Grandma Vinnie led me to the corner of the room, where a wooden platform showcased a brown piano. Sitting down, she softly sang a hymn. Emotionlessly, I stood by her side.

I must have fallen asleep on the drive home because suddenly my eyes opened wide, instantly alert. Filled with dread, I wondered if God was trying to tell me something.

The following day, we arrived early at the hospital. As soon as we entered Daddy's room, I saw him lying piteously in bed. The unnerving sight of tubes and bandages connected to his body brought me to tears. There's an old saying that a girl's father is her first love. In that moment, I realized it was true.

Despite trying to be hopeful, my heart sank when two burly men in white uniforms walked into the room. They were taking him down for X-rays, so the nurse led us back to the waiting area. Several hours later, we returned to Daddy's room. When we opened the door, I was shocked to see him sitting up in bed with a radiant smile adorning his face, lighting up the entire room. *Is this the same man we had just seen a few hours ago?* I thought.

> **Old things have passed away, behold all things have become new.**
>
> —2 CORINTHIANS 5:17 (NKJV)

With indescribable excitement, my father started telling the story of what had happened the night before. He said the doctor informed him, "Mr. Bridges, the tube we placed into your side was too small, so we're going to operate again in the morning."

Daddy vividly described the excruciating pain of the operation. So, in the quiet of the night, he bowed his head and prayed, "Lord, if you dry up this fluid in my lungs, I'll leave this hospital a new man." The next day, while we waited down the hall, the doctor had walked into his room and said, "Mr. Bridges, we don't know what has happened, but the fluid in your lungs is no longer there!"

I could hardly contain the overwhelming feeling of joy and thankfulness. And despite the doctor's lack of understanding, I knew precisely what had happened. In a moment of quiet desperation, my father had cried out to God, and God had responded to his plea.

Daddy remained at the hospital for a few more days. Each day, during our visits, he would dismiss everyone from the room except for me. Once we were alone, he would softly request me to read the Bible to him. It became my greatest joy.

Just as he said he would, my father emerged from the hospital a man reborn. The old George Bridges had died and was now a new creation in Christ Jesus!

Shortly after Daddy's spiritual awakening, my younger brother, Lance, felt the divine calling and devoted his life to God. He was ten years old.

I finally knew the hidden meaning of my dream as both Daddy and Lance left their old selves and became servants of God.

I Remembered Your Prayer

Allison Lynn

My mother says I could sing before I could speak.

From my earliest days, I joined every music group that would let me in the door. I played piano, guitar, trumpet, and even steel drums. I sang in choirs and acted in school musicals. Performing was deep in my soul, and I took every opportunity to revel in that joy.

I daydreamed of being on stage and singing for adoring crowds, but pursuing a career in music seemed unrealistic. The adults in my life were teachers, lawyers, and clergy. Professional musicians were on the radio or in music videos. No one in my world made their living in music.

Thankfully, I had another passion—a more realistic passion. I loved caring for children.

The year my friends and I turned thirteen, our church offered a babysitting course. For 6 weeks, we learned how to warm bottles, change diapers, and handle any toddler-related emergency. Certificates in hand, we were unleashed into the congregation as hirable sitters.

My evenings were soon filled by parents eager for a night on the town. I took my job seriously. No guests, no phone calls. I was a professional, even at thirteen!

I still loved music, but as high school moved forward, a career pathway started to unfold before me.

Most of the children I worked with came from loving, stable homes, just like me. But along the way, I'd learned of the horrors of child abuse. My tender heart was crushed by the stories I'd heard. I couldn't imagine how someone could contemplate causing harm to a child, much less inflicting it.

I couldn't stop the abuse, but maybe I could do something to help the healing.

As my plan became clear, I offered it up to God. "Lord, it breaks my heart that so many of your little ones are abused, broken, and violated. Help me become a child psychologist so that I may help them heal and live beautiful lives in You."

> **Take delight in the LORD, and he will give you the desires of your heart.**
>
> —PSALM 37:4 (NIV)

With that prayer in my heart, I entered university and declared psychology as my major.

But in my sophomore year, God knocked me off my feet. One weekend, singing Beethoven in a grand choral concert, I had an epiphany. It was as clear a moment as I'd ever had. It was like God was saying to me, "You're an artist. You've always been an artist. I want you to pursue performing for your career."

I was dumbstruck. This wasn't the plan. I mean, yes, becoming a singer was my dream, but it was my wild, unrealistic, over-the-top dream. It wasn't practical.

But if God calls us to something, who are we to judge what's practical?

I took a deep breath. I thanked God for all the opportunities He'd given me to care for His little ones. Then, I took that prayer and carefully tucked it away like a keepsake.

The next day, I told my parents what had happened. I changed my major and started to follow God's new calling on my life.

Soon, my days were filled with creativity, song, and adventure. I performed in musicals, sang with a big band, and even acted in films. Every day I felt blessed beyond measure to live my artistic life.

It's notoriously tough to make a living as an artist, especially in your early years. Most of my friends waited tables to make ends meet. I, on the other hand, had another skill in my pocket.

I started teaching music classes for young children. It was my perfect day job. I taught every morning and filled my afternoons and evenings with rehearsals and performances. It was busy, but I loved every moment.

After several years of teaching, the director of an uptown preschool called me into her office.

"We've received a request from a women's shelter for music classes," she said. "Would that interest you?"

"I don't see why not," I responded.

"I have to warn you," she explained. "This will be a very different teaching environment. These moms have recently escaped violent, abusive homes. Their children are suffering from PTSD and a host of other emotional challenges. You can't tell anyone where you're going, and you can never give anyone the address of the shelter. You'll need to go through a security check when you arrive."

My stomach started to twist into a knot. What was I getting myself into?

"But, Allison, I think you're a great fit for this. Your gentle style will be a real blessing for these families."

A few days later, I nervously entered the front doors of the shelter, carrying my guitar and a suitcase full of bells, shakers, and tambourines.

"We're so glad you're here!" The supervisor beamed. "We've never had music classes before. Our families are going to love this!"

The classroom windows faced the backyard—another effort for security. I was introduced to a group of hesitant young women. Their eyes were rimmed with the shadows of their recent stresses. The children hid behind their mommies' legs, eyeing me with wary curiosity.

Strumming a few chords, I began to sing, "Good morning, good morning to you!" The children quickly shed their inhibitions as they danced and jumped their way through the songs. The more they sang, the more the moms started to relax. For the first time in weeks, maybe months, these traumatized women were able to just be moms, singing with their children and having fun together.

> **In their hearts humans plan their course, but the LORD establishes their steps.**
>
> —PROVERBS 16:9 (NIV)

Soon, I was teaching at shelters across the city. My acting agent knew never to schedule an audition during these times. I could get a sub to cover a regular class, but I became fiercely protective of my shelter families.

One Tuesday, our gathering began like any other. This was an afterschool class where the moms could bring babies, toddlers, and older siblings together. The school-aged children loved acting as "helpers," passing out shakers and helping the babies dance. Over the weeks, the group had bonded into a sweet community.

We started with the classics—"Twinkle, Twinkle, Little Star," "Pat-a-cake," and "Head, Shoulders, Knees and Toes."

"Okay," I said with a knowing smile. "Grab your partners and get in your boat!" The room filled with cheers!

"Row, Row, Row Your Boat" had become a favorite moment in our time together. Each mom sat facing her oldest child, with their legs straight out and feet touching. As they stretched across to hold hands, the babies crawled onto their legs to board the "boat." Then they leaned back and forth, rowing their boat and singing, "Row, row, row your boat, gently down the stream . . ."

> "For I know the plans I have for you," declares the LORD, "plans to prosper you and not to harm you, plans to give you hope and a future."
>
> —JEREMIAH 29:11 (NIV)

The moms and children laughed and giggled as they rowed. The joyful noise grew and grew as we sang the song over and over again.

Suddenly, the sound in the room changed. I was still singing, they were still singing, but it was like the volume dropped. I could see and hear everyone, but the sound was muted.

I heard a voice say, "See, I remembered your prayer."

What? Who said that?

It echoed again. "I remembered your prayer."

GOD'S GIFT OF HEARING
— Tez Brooks —

WHEN STUDENTS IMMERSE themselves in recreation, teachers often try whispering to get their attention. Raising their voice doesn't help—kids don't hear it. A quiet tone causes kids to close their mouths and zero in on what adults are saying. Only then can they hear instruction or encouragement. The distraction of activity is immense for anyone. Even honorable deeds can overpower the Lord's call as He whispers, "Come and sit at my feet." God's voice is much clearer when people disconnect from emails, television, radio, and other distractions.

I looked around. Everyone was still singing, still laughing. No one else heard the voice. Just me.

Immediately, I knew it was the voice of God, and I knew the prayer.

"Lord, it breaks my heart that so many of your little ones are abused, broken, and violated. Help me become a child psychologist so that I may help them heal and live beautiful lives in You."

Within seconds, the volume in the room had returned to normal. Moms were singing and children were laughing. Babies and toddlers rolled around the floor as they playfully fell out of their boats.

The children moved into position for our closing song—a hug-filled version of "You Are My Sunshine."

I waved goodbye to all the happy faces as I packed up my guitar. I made my way outside, put my instruments in the trunk, and sat in the front seat. But I couldn't start the car. Not yet.

My mind went back to the classroom, to the voice. "I remembered your prayer."

That prayer I had tucked away. The dream I thought was over.

But here I was, almost 20 years later, living that prayer. Not in the way I'd imagined it. Not as a child psychologist, seeing clients for therapy sessions.

I wasn't walking that journey with them. Instead, together, we were singing and dancing our way into healing, hope, and joy.

As I sat in the silence of my car, tears rolled down my cheeks. I marveled at the loving way God had granted me my artist life, but had still kept this forgotten prayer alive. I looked back at the paths my life had taken and saw them all leading to this moment. I was humbled by the God who values the hidden dreams of our hearts.

I turned the key and pulled out of the parking lot, singing a song of praise. God remembered my prayer and filled it beyond anything I could ask or imagine.

Everything we experience on life's road is to move us toward greater love and charity, to make us draw closer to ourselves, closer to one another, closer to God.

—Susan L. Taylor

CHAPTER 4

Opening Hearts, Building Lives

The Least of These.........................158
   Heather Jepsen

The Bookmark.............................163
   Rhoda Blecker

The Gift of Christmas......................168
   Marsha H. Myers

Bumped to First Class.....................174
   Laurie Davies

Her Pattern Was Love.....................180
   Roberta Messner

The Circle of Life..........................186
   Leanne Jackson

At Home with Friends.....................190
   Stacey Thureen

The Least of These

Heather Jepsen

Last year my church started a ministry to the homeless. We are not a big church, and we are not in a big city. This is no downtown soup kitchen or famous gospel mission. This is just a little church in a small town that has a lady with a big heart.

Martha is one of the longtime members at our church who used to work at the university in our town. She was a big deal at the university's business school, all numbers and profits, and when she retired, she wanted to give back. She started working with some other community leaders to begin "Journey Home," a homeless shelter that works to move people into permanent housing.

We are the county seat, with a train stop and a bus stop, so we are a place where lots of people just end up. In the past 5 years the face of our little downtown has really changed. Many residents don't quite know what to do with those who turn up here with no resources.

There is a strong divide in our community between those who want to help the homeless and those who would rather those folks simply move along. From changing the rules about who can be in the library, to removing all the benches in the downtown area, there has been a lot of activity to discourage the homeless from staying in our town. While it is true that some homeless folks can be disruptive, we also have lots of young people and families that are simply down on their luck. Folks don't mean any harm—they just have nowhere to go.

Our two overnight shelters close during the day, so homeless people have nowhere to be from eight in the morning until five at night, when the shelters open up. Martha came to me, the pastor at our church, last year and asked if we could host these people at the church 1 day a week. She said we weren't using very much of the building during the week, and she promised she would monitor everyone and keep things safe.

> **And do not forget to do good and to share with others, for with such sacrifices God is pleased.**
>
> —HEBREWS 13:16 (NIV)

I was going to need to convince my board of elders that helping the homeless was a good use of our resources. Plus, I knew with a project of this size that I was going to need buy-in from the whole church. As you might imagine, it was a tough sell. Many parishioners did not want homeless individuals hanging out at the church at all. In fact, earlier in that same year we had to block off our back staircase because people were sleeping down inside it and leaving a mess. I wasn't sure I would be able to help Martha with this project, but I was committed to trying.

I introduced the idea with a sermon on Matthew 25. Jesus tells us that however we treat those in need is how we treat Him. Those who are hungry, without shelter or clothing, are the ones who are living as Jesus in our midst. Could we as a church community stand by and watch these people suffer without trying to help just a little bit? Or could we manage to open our doors and our hearts 1 day a week?

The Lord moved and Martha got approval for her mission, but not everybody was happy about it. Dan, one of the church trustees, cares a lot about the building and has invested a lot of time and energy into the church community, but he can be a little grumpy. Plus, as an ex-parole officer, he has seen his fair share of folks who were up to no good.

As the mission began, I would often see Dan at the church. "Hey, Dan," I would say, "Are you coming to help with the homeless lunch?"

"No!" he'd answer gruffly. "I just want to make sure nothing is getting messed up."

For the first 3 months of the mission Dan was there every Tuesday, checking on the building and the people. He never stayed more than a few minutes.

> **Give to everyone who asks you, and if anyone takes what belongs to you, do not demand it back.**
>
> —LUKE 6:30 (NIV)

Time went on and the homeless ministry expanded. Partnering with other agencies in the community, we were able to offer free or reduced-cost health care and dental. Food was acquired from the local food bank, and community volunteers prepared meals. My church kept busy providing the warm space, storage for necessary items, and free Wi-Fi. Before long, we were seeing 30 to 50 people a day, and the church board agreed to expand the mission to 2 days a week. The resources to help the homeless community were there, and we were able to provide a central place for everything to happen.

As the pastor I was aware that there were some growing pains. Even though Martha was doing her best, every now and then we would find something broken or missing. And there was still a divide in the church between those who were willing to help with the homeless ministry and those who still weren't sure it was such a good idea. You can guess which side Dan was on.

So I couldn't have been more surprised when 6 months into our homeless ministry, Dan told a story at a trustees meeting.

> **Share with the Lord's people who are in need. Practice hospitality.**
> —ROMANS 12:13 (NIV)

Contractors working in town had left a giant hole in our lawn, right next to the sidewalk, and we were concerned someone would accidentally step in the hole, twist their ankle, and get hurt. Dan had been tasked with filling the large hole with gravel. About 100 yards from the hole was a gravel area that used to be a playground for a now-defunct church preschool. The trustees decided we could use the gravel to fill the hole. Dan volunteered to take care of it even though it would take quite a few trips by wheelbarrow.

As he was filling the hole, Dan was approached by a stranger. The man said he didn't know Dan but he did know our church. He was homeless and had eaten lunch at our church more than once. He asked Dan if he could do the work for him as a way of paying us back. Dan said yes.

This homeless fellow spent the afternoon shoveling gravel and pushing the wheelbarrow back and forth to help out the church. Dan monitored him and confirmed that he did the job well. At the end of the day as they shook hands, Dan's thoughts about the homeless ministry had changed.

Although Dan is still not 100 percent on board with all our homeless work, his heart was softened toward the homeless community through the simple language of hard work. Maybe these folks did have something to offer the church after all.

As a pastor my heart was touched as well. I know Scripture tells us to serve, but I have never seen it myself in such a profound way. Jesus is in us when we help the homeless just as Jesus is in the homeless when they receive help. And Jesus is especially present when we all help one another. In Matthew 25:40 (NIV), Jesus says, "Truly I tell you, whatever you did for one of the least of these brothers and sisters of mine, you did for me," and we never know how those words might change our lives.

The Bookmark
Rhoda Blecker

My conference in Vancouver, British Columbia, wasn't due to start for another couple of hours, so I did what I always do when I'm on my own in an unfamiliar city—I looked up the nearest bookstore and headed over. Browsing in a bookstore is one of my favorite ways to spend time when I'm early for anything, and one of the reasons is because I love bookmarks with cats on them. I've bought cat bookmarks in American stores from Arizona to Massachusetts and in European stores from Basil Blackwell in Oxford to Vatican City. I am an indefatigable consumer.

I think I got started buying bookmarks in bookstores because it was a way to pay for the hours of browsing without buying any books, because books cost a great deal more, and because my "to be read" pile was taller than I was—and still is, though the titles have changed over the years. So my venture into that Vancouver bookstore was aimed at finding more cat bookmarks, after several hours of toying with old favorite volumes being reprinted and discovering new releases by authors whose work I enjoyed.

When I looked at my wristwatch and saw that I was nearing the time to leave for the opening reception of the conference, I dove into the bookmarks, of which this bookstore had a great many. Some of the nature ones caught my attention—a bookmark featuring the walls of the Grand Canyon around the granaries at Nankoweap and another of Deer Creek Falls, both places I knew well from my Colorado River trips—but they were not the kind I always bought, so I put them aside. This particular store had a huge selection of bookmarks with pithy sayings on them, and that was intriguing enough that I spent more time than I should have reading the wise or funny or nonsensical advice before I concentrated on choosing some new cat bookmarks for my collection.

> **You cannot foresee the actions of God, who causes all things to happen.**
>
> —ECCLESIASTES 11:5 (JPS)

I chose three, two with a single cat (a tabby and a Siamese), and one with three Bengals who looked as if they were deigning to pose for an inferior photographer. I got in line at the cash register to pay for them. But something I couldn't quite explain made me step out of line and go back to the bookmark display to look again at the stacks with the sayings on them. It felt like I was being called by one of the bookmarks, and I soon found the one that was beckoning me.

It looked nothing at all like any bookmark I had ever bought before. It had a solid beige background, without any design or graphic element, only the words, in black block letters, reading, "Chase your dreams, but always know the road that will bring you home again." I was confused about why I'd focused on it, because it didn't apply to me at all. My husband, Keith, and I lived just across the Canadian border, in Washington State. I'd been there in the morning, before I drove up to Vancouver for the meeting, and I'd be going home in 2 days, when the conference was over. I wasn't chasing a dream; I was working. And I probably could have gotten home with one eye closed and one hand tied behind my back.

I couldn't have said what compelled me to pick up that particular bookmark, but I added it to my other three and got back in line to pay. When I got to my car, I put the four bookmarks into the briefcase with all my conference materials and drove back to the hotel, just in time for the welcome reception.

> **You shall know that I have been sent to you by the LORD of Hosts.**
>
> —ZECHARIAH 6:15 (JPS)

The reception was in one of the suites, a charming, cozy spot with plush chairs and couches in small groups and several long tables containing trays of the kind of refreshments that would be served at high tea. I parked my briefcase in one of the chairs to stake it out, then went to the buffet for a tray and food. They were serving liquor in addition to the standard beverages, but I passed it up for tea, to stay with the overall British theme of the place.

When I returned to my chair with the tray, which I unloaded onto a small coffee table that served this particular group of seats, there was a young man in the chair next to it, sipping an amber liquid that I couldn't identify, but was sure was alcoholic. We smiled at each other, and he put his drink on the table, rose, and took my tray.

"I'll take this back for you," he said.

I thanked him, and when he came back and sat down, retrieving his glass, we introduced ourselves and chatted about the upcoming presentations and panels. But then the

GOD'S GIFT OF TASTE
— Kim Taylor Henry —

TASTE IS ONE of the many gifts of God that, to reap its full blessing, requires one to slow down and focus on what one's taste buds are experiencing. When we gobble and eat hastily or without attention, we miss out on much of the gift of taste, for flavor is meant to be savored.

Similarly, when we rush through life and do not take the time to focus on or pay attention to Jesus, the Bread of Life, much of what He offers is missed. Slowing down and savoring the experience of being with Him brings the greatest rewards.

---

conversation ran down, and he got a momentary, faraway look. Then he launched into a more personal story, the words spilling out as if he'd been holding them in for a long time. I had the impression that he was feeling safe telling it to a stranger he wouldn't see again when the conference was over.

He had gone to law school in Massachusetts, passed the bar in New York, and lived there, vacationing in Europe or Asia for the better part of 20 years at that time, while his older brother and sister stayed in Campbell River, a small city on Vancouver Island where his family had had a business for several generations. His decision to strike out for himself had been unpopular with his family, so it led to a long estrangement, only now coming to an end. He had chosen to use this conference as an excuse to return to Canada, and when it was over, he was going to see how Campbell River had changed since he left.

I wondered if he was really saying "to see how my family has changed." I didn't know him well enough to ask such an intrusive question, but somehow I knew I had been guided to this spot, and I had a mission to fulfill. I opened my briefcase, took out the cat-less bookmark, and handed it to him, saying, "I think I got this for you."

He was still holding it when the reception broke up. And even though we hadn't spoken about faith during our long conversation, I had yet another opportunity to marvel at the way that God works to bring comfort to everyone, no matter where their journey takes them.

> **A man's gift eases his way.**
>
> —PROVERBS 18:16 (JPS)

The Gift of Christmas
Marsha H. Myers

What began as an effort to rebuild my life turned into a journey that restored my faith.

Mom and I had made it through some tough times the previous year and decided to plan a road trip from South Texas, where we lived, to Northern Oklahoma, a 720-mile trip to celebrate with family on Christmas. This was going to be our gift to each other. Planning the trip and finding the resources to make it happen were going to require the kind of hope and faith that could move mountains.

It all began when I started the arduous task of figuring out how to put my life back together after a very painful divorce and moving in with my mom. For her part, she was still dealing with the painful memories of my brother's death several years before. Time was slowly passing by, and I continued to pray for guidance and direction to begin creating a new life for myself.

Early one morning, as I was sitting out on the balcony of my mom's tiny apartment, drinking coffee and talking with the Lord, my precious sister-in-law called. She excitedly told me about a scholastic grant she had just received to attend college in the town where she lived. She suggested I apply for a grant at the same school and offered me room and board if it was approved. It was an amazing offer—a blessing I couldn't pass up. So I applied for the grant, and was ecstatic when I learned it was approved. Meanwhile, I also learned that the college offered a work program for their students. So I applied for a job and was hired to tutor students during the week and also found a second job working on the weekends.

All my prayers for guidance and direction to rebuild my life had literally been answered. I was moving forward on my new life.

Finally, the day for our Christmas road trip had arrived! Mom and I were so excited we couldn't stop smiling. As we drove along the Dallas freeway in my MG Midget, it was funny to see the look of total disbelief plastered on everyone's face when they drove past us. I'm pretty sure people thought we were a couple of nuts grinning from ear to ear, driving in a car the size of a child's battery-operated toy.

We had been traveling all day and our destination was only 222 miles away when an unexpected winter storm developed. We couldn't believe it. There'd been no warning of bad weather on the radio. Soon icy rain and snow began to come down hard and fast, and the freeway was getting covered. Ice was building up on the windshield and it was hard to see. It quickly became unsafe for us to continue to drive, so I focused on finding an exit that offered some kind of shelter.

Suddenly, the engine started acting up. It was making a weird noise and was occasionally cutting out. I pulled the car

> **And not only so, but we glory in tribulations also: knowing that tribulation worketh patience, and patience, experience: and experience, hope.**
>
> —ROMANS 5:3–4 (KJV)

over to the shoulder before it stopped running completely, put on the hazard lights, and stepped out into the storm. I tried to open the hood, hoping that someone would see and stop to help us, but there was so much snow and ice covering the car, the hood was frozen shut. I got back inside the car and told Mom I had to go and try to find us some help. We joined hands, bowed our heads, and prayed for the Lord God to help us.

As I prepared to leave, fear bombarded my mind and I was overcome with doubt about leaving my mom alone. It was very cold inside the car so I tried restarting it to leave the heater running while I was gone, but it would not start. I recalled an exit we'd passed about a quarter mile back, so I made up my mind to walk back there and find some help. As I started getting ready to leave, I began talking to myself and reciting scriptures out loud to try to regain my composure. I knew in my heart it was time to leave, and I put on my hat, coat, and gloves, then bundled Mom up with the blanket I'd thought to pack at the last minute.

I stepped back out into the storm. I started walking to the back of the car to try to hitch a ride to the nearest phone (this was long before cell phones). Then out of nowhere a tow truck pulled up. A very tall, large gentleman stepped out and approached me. I wasn't at all nervous. Rather, I was grateful! I was ready to cry at this point as I told him that the engine was acting up and that my mom was in the car, and we desperately needed help.

After he calmed me down, he told me he would be glad to help us out. He walked past me, opened the car door, and helped Mom out, then guided us back to his truck, instructing us to hop in and get warm while he checked out the problem.

Eventually, he came back and told us he would have to tow the car to his shop to get a better look at the engine. I explained to him we didn't have very much money and that we would not be able to pay him for his help. I asked him if he would just take us to use a pay phone instead. But he insisted that we allow him to tow the car to his shop, partly because he needed to get us out of that very dangerous situation. Finally we relented, and he hooked up the car and off we went.

On the way to his shop we chatted about our goal to celebrate Christmas with our family and how grateful we were for his help. He understood why it was so important for us to reach our destination. Clearly this man had been sent by God.

When we reached his shop, Mom and I went inside, the warmth of the office and smell of hot coffee making us feel safe. The tow truck driver told us to make ourselves at home and to use the phone to call our family and let them know about our situation. He left to go check the engine. It wasn't long before he came back into the office to tell us that he'd located the problem and was able to repair it. We offered to pay him as much as we could for all he had done to help us, but he refused to accept it and told us it was a gift; he said to go and visit our family for Christmas. After again thanking him—and God—we set out on our way.

> **And the LORD, he it is that doth go before thee; he will be with thee, he will not fail thee, neither forsake thee: fear not, neither be dismayed.**
>
> —DEUTERONOMY 31:8 (KJV)

GOD'S GIFT OF SMELL
— Kimberly Shumate —

"WALK IN THE way of love, just as Christ loved us and gave himself up for us as a fragrant offering and sacrifice to God" (Ephesians 5:2, NIV). Such a loving image, that Jesus's sacrifice was a scent so pleasing to the Father that He applied it to us in the shadow of the cross. And while our physical bodies are but "the grass of the field" (Matthew 6:30, NIV), here today and gone tomorrow, God knows we are a spiritual perennial, our souls reborn so they can bloom. Christ's eternal perfume carries us upward to Him—within the beautiful scent of our surrender.

In just those couple of hours the weather had cleared and the highways had been plowed and treated. As Mom and I approached the area where our car had started to act up, we could see flares and flashing lights from police vehicles, ambulances, and fire trucks. As we drove by slowly, the scene was surreal and gut-wrenching. We saw twisted and mangled vehicles all over the highway and debris scattered everywhere. Police officers and firemen were directing traffic around the wreckage. To our astonishment, we recognized some of the more distinctive vehicles in the accident as ones that had driven past us on the highway earlier that day.

It was then I recalled what the gentleman who had repaired our car told us. The only thing wrong with my car was that the fuel line had come loose. He'd simply had to put the hose back on and tighten up a screw. That's when Mom and I realized that

God had revealed His presence multiple times. If the car had not malfunctioned when it did and the tow truck driver had not arrived when he did, we could have been involved in that horrible accident. We knew in our hearts that Almighty God had heard our prayer and sent His angel to rescue us.

As we celebrated the true gift of Christmas with our family, we thanked God not only for His son but also for His angel in the tow truck.

> **For he shall give his angels charge over thee, to keep thee in all thy ways.**
>
> —PSALMS 91:11 (KJV)

Bumped to First Class
Laurie Davies

"Here's your boarding pass, Laurie," the ticketing agent said, sliding a piece of paper across the counter.

"Oh, thanks. I already have one," I said, cradling my phone to my ear while trying to shove my book into the side of my carry-on bag.

"I printed you a new one," she said.

I should have paid attention to her tone. Looking back, I think her expression revealed she knew something I didn't.

I assumed my gate had changed. Plus, I was too tired to worry about it. I just wanted to get home to Phoenix. Flying to Montana a few days earlier had been a nightmare. Canceled flights and connections on the way to my dear friend's wedding left me scrambling and worried I'd miss the ceremony.

At the eleventh hour a seat had opened up on a flight that deposited me 200 miles southeast of my destination. My luggage didn't make it until the morning of the wedding. I got to the ceremony with 30 minutes to spare.

I somehow managed to spill that entire story to the ticketing agent for my trip home while she glanced at my license and typed away on her keyboard.

I was right.

She knew something I didn't know.

I arrived at the gate and looked more closely at my boarding pass. I thought it was some kind of mistake. Seat 2A. First class!

I boarded the plane, giddy with excitement over sitting in the second row. So much elbow room! And oh my goodness, a footrest!

"Ma'am, can I bring you a drink?" the flight attendant offered.

"But don't we do that later, after takeoff?" I wondered out loud.

She smiled. "It would be my pleasure to bring you a beverage of your choice now. I'll just come collect your glass before we taxi," she said.

My beverage arrived in a real glass. I stared out the window with a silly grin on my face.

God, this is over the top. You are so good. What did I do to be lavished with such favor today?

> **Therefore encourage one another and build each other up, just as in fact you are doing.**
>
> —1 THESSALONIANS 5:11 (NIV)

"Excuse me . . . miss?" The terse tone jolted me out of my fairy tale. The man in seat 4D called out to the flight attendant. "I ordered my drink without ice. Would you bring it the way I ordered it, please?"

His "please" didn't mean *please*. It meant *now*.

The flight attendant apologized and came hurriedly to collect his drink.

"Sheesh. How hard is it to actually listen?" the man complained to no one in particular. He snapped his magazine tight, read a few lines, and breathed a heavy sigh before continuing. "There's, like, five of us in first class today. Doesn't seem like it would have been too hard for her to get it right. Incompetence is everywhere."

As the flight attendant closed in on his seat with a freshly poured drink, I knew she was in earshot of those demeaning remarks.

"Here you go, sir. Enjoy," she said.

She's got an unworldly amount of poise, I thought to myself.

Now soaring to our cruising altitude, the pilot directed our attention to the left side of the plane to the summit of Mount Rainier. I'm not sure it looked any more majestic from first class, but I know the seat was so wide I physically had to scoot over just to get a good view.

I sighed a happy sigh.

> **I will bless you . . . and you will be a blessing to others.**
>
> —GENESIS 12:2 (NLT)

"Would you like chicken, beef, or vegetarian today?" the flight attendant asked, pulling my attention back into the cabin.

"There's a meal? I could cry right now," I told her. "I didn't have time to eat dinner in Seattle."

She smiled and waited for my order.

"Chicken," I said.

I felt a strong nudge from the Lord to leave my computer in my carry-on bag and look for an opportunity to pay His kindness forward. I started praying about a moment to encourage the flight attendant. I thanked her at every turn, especially for picking up my linen napkin and empty plate.

After serving everyone, she headed toward the front galley.

"Would you like to join me?" I invited her, nodding to the empty seat next to me.

"Oh, I can't, but thank you," she said, leaning over the row and indicating with her left knee resting on the empty seat that she might, however, enjoy a chat.

We talked about our kids and hometowns. We were both Midwesterners. We both pivoted to start new careers in our forties.

"Is this your first time in first class?" she asked.

I shifted my weight in my seat. "Am I that obvious?"

"Yes," she said. "And it's fun. I think people miss the fun of it all sometimes."

I asked her the question that had been on my mind during our twenty minutes of small talk. I asked her if she was a Christian.

"I knew it," she exclaimed. "I knew you were a Christian!"

> **Therefore, whenever we have the opportunity, we should do good to everyone—especially to those in the family of faith.**
>
> —GALATIANS 6:10 (NLT)

She didn't even answer my question. She didn't have to. Our conversation turned quickly to matters of faith and how our adult kids were making their faith their own. We agreed it was beautiful and also sometimes hard to watch—because they were learning big lessons the same way we did when we were younger: by messing up.

"Miss?"

The tone was less terse, yet still unmistakable. The man in 4D needed a drink.

"*No ice*," I mouthed, making a back-and-forth cut gesture at my neck. She giggled, took a new round of orders through the cabin, collected trash, and returned to her perch over my row. I nodded again toward the empty seat next to me.

She propped her same knee up on the seat, this time half-sitting.

Our conversation deepened, as we opened up about what God was teaching us in the new empty nest phases of our lives. We compared notes on what it means to live a life of faith in our fifties compared to what we thought it meant in our thirties.

"I wish I'd had more humility then," she said.

I nodded knowingly.

"I want you to know," I said quietly, "that the way you handled the man in 4D was classy. I'm sorry he talked about you that way. But God will honor you for treating others with dignity even when they don't do that for you. You're doing a good job."

She nodded thanks and mumbled something about needing to start preparing the cabin for landing.

We were still an hour from Phoenix.

I think she was dabbing at her eye.

Finally, 30 minutes later, the flight attendant announced it was time for seat backs to be returned to their upright position. It occurred to me for the first time that I had been so comfortable I had never even reclined.

Next time, I thought, giggling because I was on pace for that to happen around the year 2075.

Once safely at the gate, I gathered my things and looked around for the flight attendant. I didn't see her. I really wanted to say goodbye.

She emerged from the galley just as I passed.

"Thank you," I said, mock-straightening my posture and smoothing my skirt. "You made me feel first class today."

"No," she said, stepping just slightly in front of me to stop me—and the entire line of people behind me. "You made *me* feel first class today."

We hugged.

Funny, I thought, as I walked up the jet bridge. My seat upgrade hadn't been about me at all. God had His eye on another one of His children—one who needed to know that she was doing a good job. One who needed to feel honored.

One who needed to feel first class.

Her Pattern Was Love
Roberta Messner

On that sweltering July afternoon, I found myself sitting on the edge of a hopelessly threadbare sofa trying to dodge a protruding spring. At my mother's insistence, I'd come to deliver a bag of fresh produce and a few dozen eggs to a woman named Esther. Mom had learned about her on the bulletin board at the Big Bear grocery store.

"Esther helps homeless folks build a new life," Mom said. "If she doesn't get donations, they don't have a good meal." While it sounded like a noble cause, I tried my best to weasel out of the errand. I was busy with a photo shoot for the cover of a big home décor magazine. Then Mom gave me that look, and I promised to swing by Esther's on the way to the shoot.

Never in my wildest thoughts could I have imagined Esther. When I arrived, the door to her tenement apartment was propped open with an institutional-size can of green beans. Esther herself welcomed me from the cookstove. Her gray hair was bobby-pinned into a bun and her chocolate-colored skin was shiny with sweat. She wore only a yellowed nylon slip. Her bare foot stroked a dog's belly as she stirred the day's fare in a huge silver pot. The place smelled like a roadside farm stand.

I figured I needed to strike up some sort of conversation. After I introduced myself, I focused my attention on the object of Esther's affection. "What kind of dog is that?" I asked.

A toothless smile filled her face. "Why, honey, I've got myself a gen-u-wine West Virginia brown dog," she said. "Turned up at my door one day like the rest of my fixer-uppers."

What in heaven's name was a West Virginia brown dog? *Must be one with no particular provenance,* I decided. *Much like this forsaken place.*

The all-purpose room where Esther fed her "fixer-uppers," with its shabby, mismatched couches lining the walls, was a world away from the homes I styled for the camera's eye. In my mid-30s, I'd become pretty pleased with the direction my life had taken. I had goals, dreams. I checked them off the list in my purse with pride.

Just then a tall, skinny guy popped his head inside the room. "Been 34 days since I used, Mama Esther," he announced.

Esther smiled bigger than ever at that news. "Just keep trusting God, Bubba," she said. "You're gonna make it for sure. And by the way, we're having scrambled eggs and vine-ripened tomatoes tonight. Peek inside that poke. This nice lady here brought them."

> **By this everyone will know that you are my disciples, if you love one another.**
>
> —JOHN 13:35 (NIV)

Soon the skinny guy was on his way and the hand-lettered sign above Esther's stove took on new meaning: "Love Covers a Multitude of Thins."

Esther caught me reading her words. "Most of my fixer-uppers are like Bubba," she explained. "I just try to include everybody and put a little meat on their bones." She went on to tell me that Bubba had two little ones. "He's been doing well enough lately to walk them over to the Piggly Wiggly," she said. Her voice dropped to a confidential whisper.

"Now, they're not supposed to do this, but there's a cashier who lets his kids ride the conveyor belt. They've never been to an amusement park or anything, so it's a big thrill."

With that little tidbit, Esther was off and running. She told me about Sonny, who used to camp out on the riverbank in Tent City. About Art, Pokey, Babes, and Cath. And about a waif named Abby who'd once been manager of a fabric store. She'd fallen on hard times, lost her job *and* her husband, and ended up living in her car. Of course that was before Esther and God came into her life.

> **And over all these virtues put on love, which binds them all together in perfect unity.**
>
> —COLOSSIANS 3:14 (NIV)

As I rose from the sofa to leave, I had a real appreciation for all Esther was trying to accomplish. Still, I couldn't help but wonder about Esther as a person. She devoted her every minute to these former street people who lived in her building. Portioned out their medications every morning. Fed them. Looked after all their needs. But what about *her*?

"Esther," I said, thinking of the list in my purse. "What you do here is amazing. But do you have any dreams just for *you*?"

Esther's brown eyes took on a faraway look and she turned down the heat on the stove. The next thing I knew she was crawling on the floor and pilfering under one of the sofas.

Her search brought up a bent cardboard box. "I don't usually tell people this," she said, "especially those I've just met. But I do have a dream." She pulled out a piece of crochet work not much bigger than a pot holder. "I'd like to make me a blanket big enough to stretch around this whole room. Thanksgiving will be here before we know it, and it's going to get drafty in here. If I had that blanket, I could keep everyone warm while they eat."

The small, crocheted square had no rhyme or reason to it. Esther had used every color in the Crayola box and the strangest stitches I'd ever seen. Ticking off some names I'd heard my grandmother and her needle-art friends discuss, I asked her: "Esther? What pattern *is* this? Granny square? Ripple stitch? Dragonfly?"

"None of those fancy things," Esther said with a chuckle. "I just made do with what I had until I ran out of yarn. Only pattern I know is love."

I had nothing to say to that, but Esther was still thinking about her dream. "Tell you what. If you ever find yourself in one of those Goodwill places and can pick me up some yarn real cheap, I sure would like that. The colors can be all different. Just like the people who come here."

All day long at the shoot I couldn't help thinking about Esther. Especially when I nearly got lost going from room to room. "This is a great house for a man who doesn't want to run into anybody," the designer told me as he forced a laugh.

It's a world away from Esther's crowded apartment, I thought.

On my way home I stopped at Goodwill, but there was no yarn to be had. I decided to try Kmart. There I happened upon a Blue Light Special where three shelves of yarn were going for ten cents a skein! I loaded two buggies with every last one of them. Red. Green. Blue. Yellow. One of the clerks had to help me to the register.

Filled with an excitement I hadn't known in ages, I headed straight for Esther's. She was doing up the dinner dishes, but she squealed and dropped a Melmac bowl when she spotted all the yarn. Dishes forgotten, she immediately began to put that yarn to use. Her nimble fingers flew as she added a red patch to the little crocheted square. Watching her work totally fascinated me. When my grandmother had once tried to teach me to crochet, I couldn't get the hang of winding the yarn around my index finger like you were supposed to do. It had taken me 3 months to finish a simple scarf.

> **Offer hospitality to one another without grumbling.**
>
> —1 PETER 4:9 (NIV)

In the coming months I dropped in to visit Esther and to watch her blanket grow. The week of Thanksgiving I took her some more provisions.

"We've gotten us enough donations to have a real turkey feast with all the trimmings," she told me. "Please say you'll come. At least for pumpkin pie."

On Thanksgiving evening Esther hovered over her stove stirring a pot of something that smelled delicious. All of her fixer-uppers sat elbow to elbow on the threadbare couches. That much hadn't changed. But in addition to balancing plates on their laps, each one now sported a big black paper hat with a golden buckle. Esther's colorful blanket stretched around the room as she had dreamed.

I admired Esther's handiwork, surprised to see her metal crochet hook was threaded through the stitches. "You got your blanket finished," I said. "But you didn't tie it off."

"Oh, it'll never be *done*," she said. "You don't know when one more might show up. Like you today."

I found my place at the end of one of the couches and got cozy under Esther's blanket. When a spring poked my leg, I

GOD'S GIFT OF SIGHT
— Terrie Todd —

IS ANYTHING ON earth brighter than sunlight sparkling on freshly fallen snow? It's so bright, in fact, that skiers must wear goggles and sunscreen to protect their vision and skin. Despite the danger, the unsurpassed beauty of nature's winter display causes telltale tanning on a skier's face. In the same way, when we spend time with God, His beauty and glory will be reflected in us for the benefit of others. As Exodus 34:29 (NIV) reminds us: "When Moses came down from Mount Sinai . . . he was not aware that his face was radiant because he had spoken with the LORD."

---

scooted in closer to little Abby. Esther placed a piece of pumpkin pie on my lap and plopped a big black hat on my head.

"Donations, don't you know. Today we're not fixer-uppers. We're pilgrims."

I marveled at the thought of it. Esther was right: We were all, every single one of us, travelers on this journey called life. Each with a unique, God-given task.

I might not ever crochet like Esther. Life has changed, and our Kmart with its Blue Light Specials is no more. But maybe—just maybe—I could hope for a heart like hers. One that stretched on to forever and welcomed the whole world.

The Circle of Life
Leanne Jackson

In the fall of 1941, when she was 13, my mother, Marion, became seriously ill. Her worried parents wiped her forehead as her fever kept climbing. She begged her mother to go to school the next day, to attend her favorite teacher's bridal shower. Marion spent that whole day with her head on her desk, only getting up to rush to the bathroom, sick at both ends. She wearily walked home and climbed back into bed.

Marion's mother, who played the organ in her church, prayed constantly for healing. They didn't have a family doctor, so she called her friend Olga. That was her first answer to prayer. Olga knew a doctor she had gone to school with, Dr. William Jamison, who had been a medical missionary to Ceylon. When war broke out in Europe, he brought his family back to Schenectady, New York, and opened his medical practice.

Dr. Jamison examined Marion and immediately recognized the typhoid fever he'd seen in Ceylon. He started her on the brand-new sulfa drug even before tests confirmed his diagnosis. Recalling it later, Mom told me, "We all thought that was providential. Another doctor might have waited around, and typhoid can easily be fatal."

Because typhoid fever is so contagious, Marion was sent to the isolation hospital in Schenectady, which had been the polio sanitorium. Her 8-year-old brother Ab watched their father carry Marion down the stairs as their mother cried. A neighbor stayed with Ab while their parents drove Marion to the hospital.

She had to stay for 4 weeks. "I heard a lot on the radio about war, but I got home before we gathered around our radio on December 7 to hear about Pearl Harbor," she recalls. Her room was across from the nurse's station and she was one of their youngest patients, so she got lots of attention. After a week she felt well enough to get out of bed, but she wasn't allowed to touch the floor due to fear of contamination. So she stood on the wheeled base of the cloth-stretched bed screen and pushed it to the window to watch for her mother, who would drive past in her nephew Bernie's aqua-colored convertible, tooting the horn that played a jaunty tune. Marion and her mother couldn't touch, but they grinned and waved.

> LORD my God,
> I called to you
> for help, and
> you healed me.
>
> —PSALM 30:2 (NIV)

After the miracle of being led to the doctor who would save Marion's life, the family wouldn't go to anyone else—but they had no idea how soon they would need his help again.

On Christmas Eve day, less than a month after she came home from the hospital, Marion fell and broke her right arm while ice-skating with her best friend, Tina. Her parents said it was a blessing that she was left-handed, but Marion didn't agree. What teenager wants a cast for Christmas? She pouted while Dr. Jamison set her arm. He gently asked, "Young lady, do you say your prayers every night?" She nodded. "Well, you better, because this could have been a very different Christmas for your family."

That jolted her right out of her childish focus on herself. She'd never heard of typhoid fever before she contracted it, and it had never occurred to her, even in the hospital, that she might have died. She hadn't realized how frightened her parents had been. Or how lucky she was to have been taken to a doctor who recognized it and knew how to treat it.

That night she thanked God for sparing her life. She began to pray every night, and some days too—not just for herself, but for other people. Looking back, she would credit that simple conversation with Dr. Jamison with expanding her heart and widening her concept of God's presence in our lives. The lesson stuck with her throughout her life.

> **You guide me with your counsel, and afterward you will take me into glory.**
>
> —PSALM 73:24 (NIV)

Years later, Dr. Jamison changed his practice to specialize in obstetrics and gynecology, but he continued to care for the women in our family, including Marion. He delivered me and, 2 years later, my sister. The passage from one generation to the next was complete when his son took over the practice. The son told Mom stories about growing up in Ceylon and remembered once having tea with his missionary father and the civil rights leader Mahatma Gandhi.

In 1970, I was a teenage "candy striper" in my white shirt and red-and-white striped pinafore, volunteering in the emergency room. I watched from the corner of the small room as an older man was wheeled in on a stretcher following a major heart attack. One of the doctors gasped, "It's Dr. Jamison!"

He opened his eyes. He turned to the cluster of interns and residents—all doctors he'd trained—and gave his final order: "Don't do me any favors, boys." Everyone in the room was in tears as his breathing slowed, then stopped. It was the end of an era, not just for my family, but for so many people whose lives Dr. Jamison had touched. As I watched, I prayed "thank you" to Dr. Jamison for his many gifts to my loved ones, and "thank You" to our beloved God for welcoming him home.

The next time Mom had a checkup with Dr. Jamison's son, they reminisced about the long history of our two families and the way the elder Dr. Jamison had saved her life as a teen and then delivered her own children, bringing a new generation into the world. Mom shared that I had prayed for him as he died. They were both in tears as she thanked the younger Dr. Jamison for his family's legacy of care.

> **I have come that they may have life, and have it to the full.**
>
> —JOHN 10:10 (NIV)

The elder Dr. Jamison was the first person I was privileged to be with at the time of death. His life inspired me to be a caregiver and his death inspired me to be a hospice nurse. As I prayed with many patients on their final journeys, I often reflected on the providence of God.

The Divine Physician, Caregiver of us all, had prepared Dr. Jamison, then guided Mom's family to him. He gave life to my mother, then to me, then helped to birth my calling. As my mother nears the end of her own earthly journey, I am honored to care for her.

The divine circle of life—and caregiving—continues.

At Home with Friends
Stacey Thureen

Any day of the week, people walk through the solid oak-framed glass doors of the community room at our local YMCA and see several senior citizens sitting around the tables. The people in the room wear bright smiles, laugh out loud, or comfort one another as the sun's rays radiate through the large east-facing windows. Although I'm about half the age of many of these beautiful individuals, I can relate to them. Being with other people is a joy.

Similar to enduring a long, blinding, blistering cold blizzard where I live in Minnesota, I was feeling distant, hard-hearted, and disconnected from so many people within our community because of Covid restrictions. It was time to reconnect with, and serve, others again.

In the fall of 2022, Bonnie, a friend and worker at the YMCA, encouraged me to get involved at the Y. Bonnie and I had crossed paths numerous times before while there. I often trained in the pool for masters swimming events. Meanwhile, she taught water aerobics to many of the lovely senior citizens in our area. Bonnie and I had delightful conversations in passing about family life and faith. Then, one day she talked with me about the spirited people who graced the community room.

"Many of these wise individuals don't get to see their children or grandchildren often. They have so much to offer, and they'd love to get to know you. And your three kids would certainly bring smiles to their faces!" Bonnie added, "There are circumstances in their lives, like family members living far away, that make it hard for them to connect. Sometimes they just need a hug, a smile, or some sort of interaction from younger people like you."

So I went home and talked about Bonnie's idea with my husband. He encouraged me to visit the community room, but I was apprehensive. So I prayed: *God, I can relate to missing family members who are far away from me. I know the heartache of wishing I could have a hug from someone close to me. But what if I don't fit in? What if I don't know how to love and serve them well, like You have commanded me? Lord, please guide me.*

> **You will show me the path of life; in Your presence is fullness of joy; at Your right hand are pleasures forevermore.**
>
> —PSALM 16:11 (NKJV)

I trusted God that maybe I needed these people, and perhaps they needed me too. So I put all the doubts aside and literally started with toddler steps. Joy, my youngest daughter who was almost 3 at the time, and I walked into the community room, where we saw Bonnie. Joy at least recognized her and was comfortable around her. Bonnie picked her up, gave her a huge hug and a treat, and introduced Joy by name to some of the other young at heart. This became a regular routine before Joy and I left the Y to go home.

About 2 months after our visits started, Bonnie announced she was going to be stepping down from her role at the YMCA.

She said she still wanted us to come into the community room whether she was there or not. We were both starting to see the impact Joy was having on our new friends. By the time Bonnie left her job, Joy was comfortable visiting the elderly in the community room—and so was I.

I asked my small group at church to pray for me and these interactions because I saw ministry opportunities, like the time I held the hand of a woman, hugged her, and offered to pray for her after she received news that her husband had been diagnosed with cancer. There were even simple ways to share God's love just by being present.

When my kids were off from school, all three of them would come with me to the Y. I could see that their childlike energy was a precious gift to the senior citizens. My son, Dane, would often share a joke he heard at school. My oldest daughter, Avery, enjoyed small talk with the young in spirit. She would talk with them about school, what songs she was learning at piano lessons, or how much she enjoyed gymnastics.

Three days a week, a smaller group of people—usually a half-dozen or so—would sit around one of the tables in the corner of the community room. These people became known as the "coffee crew." This lively bunch has always enjoyed seeing me and my children. One of the first times Joy and I interacted with the coffee crew she gave away a craft she'd made during her time in the Y childcare room. Then, I tried to give each of the crew members a hug before we left. After several more visits, Joy warmed up to them and gave them hugs too. It changed everyone's demeanor for the better.

In addition, this group was always laughing, telling a joke, or teasing one another about something. Sometimes I would go into the room by myself just to visit with them. One day, Ron walked in late because he had to get an oil leak on his car fixed. As he walked into the community room and sat down, Karen, with her New York sense of humor, asked, "So how's the leak?" Then Jerry started talking about the water leak in his house. The next thing I knew, we all were laughing hysterically about the various "leaks" we were experiencing in our lives. I piped in, "Let me tell you about how our furnace broke on Easter and our microwave broke on Christmas Eve while I was cooking dinner!"

The coffee crew was like a therapy group. We would laugh about things that we found humor and grace in, even though at the time they were stressful.

Karen and I have grown the closest of the group. Like long-lost schoolgirls from the East Coast, we've spent many days laughing at and teasing each other. She and I have reminisced about our times lived in that part of the country.

> **But as many as received Him, to them He gave the right to become children of God, to those who believe in His name.**
>
> —JOHN 1:12 (NKJV)

"I miss the bagels with a schmear of cream cheese and the pizza pies!" I said with a huge smile on my face.

"Yes, the great Italian and Greek food made by small family-owned businesses!" Karen added.

"I also miss the diversity. I miss the accents, the culture, the climate, and the scenery," I shared.

It is this deepening relationship with Karen that attests to God's presence in my life. Karen reminds me of my godmother's mom, who lived in Queens, New York. I just adored Mildred's

GOD'S GIFT OF TOUCH
— Heidi Gaul —

THOSE SPECIAL HANDS. We know every wrinkle, every freckle, and the shape of the nails. We recognize the grip when our fingers intertwine, the heat that emanates from the palm. Few things warm the heart or reassure us more than holding hands with a spouse, beloved friend, or family member. But the benefits go further. Holding hands eases pain, reduces the stress hormone cortisol, and lowers our blood pressure and heart rate. How can something so simple and natural make such a difference for our health? We can thank the Great Physician.

---

wit, wisdom, brutal honesty, and grace. God has blessed me with Karen, who is unique in her own way yet resembles these qualities that bring back good memories.

With a smile on her face and sincerity in her voice, Karen has given me big hugs. But these aren't just any hugs. These hugs are like feeling the warmth from a fireplace. They last for at least 15 seconds, long enough that we can feel our hearts beating in unison. As her 5-foot-3 frame stands to meet mine, she often leans in and whispers into my ear, "You feel like home. You're a good girl and a great mom!"

When I see these senior citizens give my three children treats, talk to them, or spoil them with their time, I'm so thankful to God for giving my kids the gift of these relationships. My kids' grandparents live far away, so they don't have the benefit of seeing them much. I've often wished my kids could have the same special relationships with their grandparents that I had with mine, who lived in a neighboring town. While these elders are not my kids' grandparents, they are some of the best people, filling a place in their hearts and mine.

It's in the moments of warm hugs, sharing stories, and witnessing answers to prayer that I know I'm a child of God. Some days I feel alone or even a little out of place living 1,200 miles from where I grew up. But my new friends, provided by God, make me feel like I am home.

> **Two are better than one, because they have a good return for their labor: If either of them falls down, one can help the other up.**
>
> —ECCLESIASTES 4:9–10 (NIV)

When there appears no light at the end of the tunnel, look around; often we are the light in the tunnel for one another. Have faith, God is working within every circumstance and person for redemption.

—Farrell Mason

CHAPTER 5

God's Goodness in Times of Sadness

Holding on Tight 198
    Susan Engebrecht
Holding on to Hope 204
    Ashley Kappel
God's Unseen Clock 208
    Susan Deitz Shumway
God's Healing Presence 213
    Peggy Eastman
The Birds 218
    Tanja Dufrene
Lasting Joy 224
    Denise Margaret Ackerman

Holding on Tight
Susan Engebrecht

Some changes ease into life while others crack routines open like an egg dropped on concrete. I'd adjusted to our RV shower with its tiny hot water tank and dimensions just right for children or at least someone much smaller than myself. I'd learned to keep a firm grip on the bar of soap. Experience taught me that when it slips away, retrieving the little stinker can cause pain, frustration, and wasted time because it doesn't take long before the water turns cold. After banging my head on the wall in my feeble attempts to recapture the escapee, I understand the importance of holding on tight.

Each summer I taught stained glass classes at the Green Lake Conference Center. Hubby and I would spend our summers in the RV at this beautiful site. One glorious day things were going well with my RV shower; even the sun shone down on me through the sunroof above. I sang along with the hymn that drifted through the doorway from the CD player in the kitchen. And then, the sound of a lawn mower changed everything.

I knew the land around the RV held hidden tree stumps, half-buried rocks, tie-downs, hoses, and cords, all of which made mowing a challenge. I'd told my husband to wait with the mowing until after I showered and dressed. Apparently, my once independent, servant-hearted helpmate decided he couldn't wait that long.

There was a strange thump sound and then sudden deafening silence. Even the CD player ceased to fill the air with praise. Though warm water continued to rain down on me, my body froze with fear. I grabbed my robe and ran to the window.

Hubby had the mower on its side and was pulling on the still-plugged-in and now-severed RV electric cord.

"Stop," I screamed. "Put the mower down and step away." His puzzled face looked up at me, but he did as commanded. After throwing some clothes on and getting him to a safe distance from the cord, I ran to the neighbor's trailer for help.

Jim leaped into action as if 50 years had melted away and said, "Stay here" as he bolted out the door. His wife wrapped her arms around me and prayed as a flood of tears poured out. Alzheimer's had severed our lake-time sanctuary lifestyle.

> Let the morning bring me word of your unfailing love, for I have put my trust in you. Show me the way I should go, for to you I entrust my life.
>
> —PSALM 143:8 (NIV)

After the cord was repaired, we sold the RV and returned to the home we'd spent the last 50 years in. Sadly, Alzheimer's was continuing to nibble away at both of our lives. Hubby could do less and I had to do more.

His servant attitude remained alive, but putting it into action caused friction. He hovered nearby wanting to help and didn't know how. For me, his help meant that things took twice as long to accomplish. I now line up plates, glasses, and silverware so he can set the table, or I let him wash dishes and put things away in creative locations. These little things are important to make him feel like he's making a contribution.

Frustration, irritation, and disappointment lurk like shadows in hidden places in both of our minds, longing to rob us of the joy found in the precious moments of togetherness.

> **Let us hold tightly without wavering to the hope we affirm, for God can be trusted to keep his promise.**
>
> —HEBREWS 10:23 (NLT)

We often stop everything, take a prayer break, and refocus just to help keep us moving through the day. There might only be time for a quick, "Lord help us" prayer. Sometimes we long to pour out our hearts, but find that words can be as difficult to hold on to as a bar of soap in the shower, leaving us feeling like we are banging our heads against a wall. As we pray, God's Word lifts us up and anchors us in the truth, encouragement, and hope found in the pages of our Bibles. God's faithfulness stabilizes us through each change.

One morning I walked into the kitchen and Hubby was poking the coffee maker with a finger. "What are you doing?" I asked.

"I want some of this, but I don't know how to get it," he replied.

After pouring him a cup, we settled down for our morning devotions. At that point he could still read. Words came slow, were hard to pronounce, and may have required some explanation, but at least he could still read our devotional scripture.

Yesterday I found him sitting in his favorite chair in front of a window with an open Bible on his lap. I filed that moment as a photo in the memory album of my mind. Learning to cherish those tiny fleeting blessings and keep them safe didn't happen all at once. I needed to preserve them and encourage others to do the same.

When people found out that Hubby had Alzheimer's, the usual response was, "I'm so sorry," and then many of them tell stories of people they knew who had the disease. These stories never have happy endings; in fact some of them are downright frightening. Yes, it is true that Alzheimer's is frightening, and I'm sorry to have had it in our lives or in the life of anyone else, but to dwell on sorrow or fear would only complicate an already bad situation.

> When I am afraid, I put my trust in you. In God, whose word I praise—in God I trust and am not afraid.
>
> —PSALM 56:3–4 (NIV)

We traveled that road awhile in the beginning of this journey. Tears and sorrow were close at hand, but they were quicksand that pulled us to the brink of despair. Misery and gloom closed in on us as surely as the walls of my Barbie doll–sized RV shower once did. Scripture, like guideposts along the road, has helped us in the journey. Psalm 121:1 reminded me to lift my eyes; and what did the eyes of my wounded soul see? The Son still shines His Light down on me.

We've learned to enjoy today and look for little blessings and joys that fall on us in the wilderness of our journey.

Sometimes that plate of muffins in the hands of a visiting friend was manna for our souls.

Psalm 62 reminds us that our hope is in the Lord, our rock, salvation, and stronghold. Because of this truth we will not be shaken. On bad days, I've been known to mutter, "I will not be shaken" over and over. Focusing on what God says rather than shadowy thoughts causes us to lift our hands in praise rather than wring them in worry. That CD player from the RV still belts out songs of praise and worship. We sing along, off-key it's true, but with joyful voices. What a wonderful discovery to find that mouths that are praising God have little room for complaining or despair.

The Alzheimer's journey is not what we would have chosen for our golden years, but looking at it as a path of discovery rather than a burden is our choice. Life changed. The pace of daily living has slowed down, thus giving us opportunity to spend quality time together as well as time to meditate and depend more deeply on the Lord. Although we became weary, the living water God provided refreshed us and the bread of His Word filled a deep longing inside us. Plus the Lord often worked through someone else to come minister to us.

A friend stopped by to take Hubby for a walk or out to breakfast so that I could take a nap or do something more creative. A tag team of men volunteered to stay with him while I attended a woman's retreat. These examples of God's love in action gave me a time of refreshment and give Hubby fellowship with brothers in the Lord.

Neighbors grabbed rakes and helped move those beautiful fallen leaves into piles on the boulevard. Laughter and memories continue to fly around a dinner table as family and friends gather. Our sons are in the process of fulfilling the commandment to honor their father and mother with thoughtfulness and welcoming us into their home. Each act of kindness is a fresh blessing that fills our days and offers the giver the opportunity to serve.

When someone tells me, "We just got a diagnosis," I know they are entering a new season of life. Frightening things are ahead for them, but I give them a hug and say, "You're not alone in this battle. The Lord God Almighty is with you. He will instruct brothers and sisters to come alongside to cheer you on. You can trust Him. Hold on tight and lean into His arms."

Holding on to Hope

Ashley Kappel

When my husband Brian and I decided to start a family, we thought it would be easy. We both grew up with siblings, and our friends were starting to have children. It seemed like everywhere I looked, there were pregnant women and young families. "It's time!" we decided, excited that nine months later we'd have a baby.

We were greatly disappointed.

When my first miscarriage happened, I leaned into God's word. I bookmarked scriptures on my work computer about loss and God's promises. I identified with Sarah, Abraham's wife, in her desire and her doubt. I heralded Rebekah's triumph (twins!). Even Samson's mom was said to be barren before bearing a son.

The words of God swirled around me, and I felt comforted, loved, emboldened, and faithful. I was just like these women; God would provide.

And then the second miscarriage happened, and while I wish the words on my lips had been "I know You are faithful," instead it was only one woeful lament: "Why?" Day after day it felt like I was surrounded by children—walking through grocery stores seeing young families, passing children on bikes on our running trail, and finding myself behind pregnant women in checkout lines. My sister announced that she was pregnant with a child who would have shared a birth month with my now-gone babe. "Why would You take this from me?" I cried again and again. In the darkness, I heard nothing back.

"If you will not change my situation, you have to change my heart," I prayed. "You have to make me want this less. I cannot want it so badly and not be able to have it. It will break me."

This would have been one of those perfect times to have a moment with God. A moment in which I heard His voice, felt His hand stilling my chaotic pleas, my bleeding heart. But in the darkness, I felt so alone, so lost, that I felt I was all I had left.

My sorrow gradually turned to anger. Who was God to deny me this? What had I done to deserve to lose this part of who I was meant to be? *If that's who God is, maybe He is not my God. How could my God of love be so heartless and cruel?*

> **Hope deferred makes the heart sick, but a longing fulfilled is a tree of life.**
>
> —PROVERBS 13:12 (NIV)

My husband and I took a break from trying to have children. I could not handle another loss. In that time, we saw specialists, had lab work done, and decided on a "maybe this will work" regimen of medications, as fertility is a tricky territory full of unknowns and variables. During this process, we discovered that while I am able to get pregnant easily, I have a very hard time holding onto the pregnancy past the first trimester. Armed with this knowledge, the doctor prescribed a cocktail of folic acid, baby aspirin, and daily injections that we hoped would help get me through those first 12 weeks.

It did.

My pregnancy was medically easy but emotionally impossible. I begged God to keep her safe, fearfully keeping my love for her at bay even as I saw her kicks moving the skin under my shirt. Opening my heart to her meant believing that she would be OK, and I wasn't ready to take that risk.

Olivia was born at thirty-nine weeks, healthy and happy. It took years to realize I'd given her a name—and a nickname—that embodied my greatest wish for her: Liv.

We were so over the moon at Olivia's safe delivery that no one had the heart to tell us she was colicky; we didn't figure that part out until much later. When she kept us up at night, we just smiled. "Cry all you want, little one. You're here!"

In time, I would realize that if God had followed my detailed timeline, my life would have been very different. My best friends, the women who I go to for everything, are the mothers of Olivia's day-care friends; we might never have met if I hadn't had Olivia at the right time. My friends and I still meet for dinner monthly to talk about the trials of grade-schooler life. My sweet baby—the one who screamed all night, never napped, and didn't sleep for longer than two hours at a stretch until after her first birthday—might

> **If we are thrown into the blazing furnace, the God we serve is able to deliver us from it, and he will deliver us from Your Majesty's hand. But even if he does not, we want you to know, Your Majesty, that we will not serve your gods . . .**
>
> —DANIEL 3:17–18 (NIV)

have broken me if I'd had her before my struggle with fertility. Instead, I adored her and cherished every minute, snuggling while she struggled to process all that was happening in the world. And I would certainly not have learned that God's grace *is* enough for me, "even if" (as my favorite verse, Daniel 3:18, says) He does not keep me from pain in the moment.

Life is full of seasons, and I have often found myself guilty of desperately seeking the next one's arrival. How I wish I could go back in time and tell twenty-something Ashley to wait, to have faith, and to enjoy the season she was in—newly married—without desperately wishing for the next—parenthood. But, as we all know, you can't tell anyone, much less your younger self, much of anything. We all have to learn those lessons as they come.

My life didn't magically get better with children. I had another miscarriage after Olivia, and it gutted me the same as the first two did. And then I had my two boys, born almost three years apart.

These days, I do my best to be a support to the women I stumble upon who are experiencing the aftermath of miscarriage. It's a heartache no one talks about, and most suffer almost entirely alone. While I cannot rush them through their sorrow, grief, heartbreak, or anger, I can assure them that God is working, He is moving, and they are whole, and worthy, and loved.

God's Unseen Clock
Susan Deitz Shumway

It was a warm summer afternoon and my day was going just like I had hoped. I was a young mother of a 3-year-old son and 5-year-old daughter. Ashley would be starting kindergarten the following week, and my parents were planning to come to see her off on her first day of school. She was the first grandchild for my parents, so there was great anticipation.

I had a busy morning with the children and had put them down for naps. My husband was home, so I went on a walk to recharge and be ready when nap time was over. After I returned home, I got a call from my pastor, Frank, who had helped me tremendously when I accepted Christ, to see if I would be attending Bible study that evening. We exchanged a few more words, and he said he was going to call and check in on my parents. We said our goodbyes, and I hung up the phone.

Within 5 minutes the phone rang again. It was Frank, but this time instead of his usual jovial self, he explained that as he was talking to my father, he heard him say, "Frank, I am so dizzy, I think I am going to pass out." Frank heard my father fall to the floor, and so he called to alert me. I called 911 and we both said we were going to my parents' house, which was about halfway between us.

I was in complete shock, but I needed to get to their home quickly. My mother was running errands, so my dad was alone.

Just as I told my husband I was going to my parents' house, my sister, completely unaware of the situation, pulled into the drive. I knew God had placed my husband at home, with the children sleeping, and now my sister was there so we could go together.

We raced to my parents' home. Frank was already there and told us to stay outside. The EMTs worked on my father and finally brought him out and put him into the ambulance. Frank and I followed the ambulance in his car, while my sister waited for my mother to arrive home from errands. As we were headed to the hospital, Frank prayed, and God calmed my spirit and gave me peace that He was with us.

> **For I, the LORD your God, will hold your right hand, saying to you, "Fear not, I will help you."**
>
> —ISAIAH 41:13 (NKJV)

When we got to the hospital I asked about my father and was told I needed to give them information to get him registered. *Oh, thank God,* I thought. *They are admitting him.* After providing the necessary details, a nurse put us in a small room and asked us to wait for the doctor, who would come and update us.

In less than a minute the door opened, and a doctor told us my father was critical. He said he would update us as soon as he could, and then he left quickly. Moments later he was back and told us my father had passed. I was beyond devastated. How could my strong and seemingly healthy father be gone? I was in complete denial. *This simply cannot be real.*

For the next several days I lived in a complete fog. I went through the motions of caring for the children, but I simply would not allow myself to believe my father was gone. When my husband and I broke the news to my children, my son said, "If I knew what you were going to tell me, I would have plugged my ears." I wish I hadn't heard those words either.

The day of my dad's calling hours and funeral came, reality stabbing me like a knife. I ached, and my heart was broken. My mother was beyond grief. She had been a stay-at-home wife and mother and was completely lost without him. She said she felt like both legs and one arm had been cut off of her.

> **I was young and now I am old, yet I have never seen the righteous forsaken or their children begging bread.**
>
> —PSALM 37:25 (NIV)

As our new life began without my father, we attempted to navigate each new day. The first day of kindergarten was bittersweet for all of us. We had planned this picture-perfect day, but of course it did not go the way we had envisioned. Dinners at my parents' home were constant reminders that there was an empty chair, and out of respect to my father, no one felt like they wanted to sit in his chair. There was such an awkwardness in the complete emptiness of that space, but as time passed, my brother decided to be the one to fill it.

Through the loss and the tragedy, different people reached out and expressed how my father had called them recently just to check up on them and say hello. It was almost as though he had been calling friends and family for the last time, even though he did not know what was about to transpire.

I experienced something similar. The day before my father's heart attack, my parents had a new garage floor poured, and

I thought it would be fun for the children to watch the big cement trucks. We'd arrived there just as the floor was being finished. After the trucks left, my father asked if he could put the children's handprints in the fresh, wet cement. Of course he could. What a great idea! One at a time, he took their little hands and placed them in the cement, then took my children over to the outside water faucet to wash their hands.

I watched silently from a distance and noticed the beauty of this moment. A papa with his two grandchildren. He washed their hands and then pulled his big blue handkerchief out of his back pocket, shook it out, and lovingly dried their hands. I felt God's presence while witnessing that tender scene. We placed the date beside the little handprints, never realizing that would be the last time I ever saw my father alive. It is a special memory of my father, one that is forever etched in my mind.

One "coincidence" after another happened in the days and weeks following my father's death. First, we realized that God had not only petitioned Frank to call my father at that specific time but also allowed my mother to be away from home so she wouldn't be alone with my father. Later, when my mother worried she wouldn't have enough money to live on, she found out that my father had made provisions in case something happened to him within 30 days of his sixty-second birthday. Dad lived 20 days past his birthday. In the first month after his passing, we counted close to twenty instances when God showed us that

> **Do not boast about tomorrow, for you do not know what a day may bring.**
>
> —PROVERBS 27:1 (NIV)

GOD'S GIFT OF SMELL
— Buck Storm —

I'VE HEARD PEOPLE say the smell of the ocean is really the living and dying of the biomass along the coastline. A quick internet search would probably tell me if this is true or not but, honestly, I don't want to know.

For me, the smell of the sea is one of the greatest things on earth. It represents the weight of vastness, the press of mystery. Freedom. A snub to the passing of time.

It's an undeniable and glorious reminder of what is greater, or Who is Greater. And the promise of what that means.

---

this was His divine plan, having worked out all the details ahead of time.

My mother was able to live out her last twenty-five years in our family home because of the financial decisions made by my father. And the greatest blessing to me is that God provided a way for me to purchase that home just a few years ago.

Although I feel my father is still protecting me, I know it is my heavenly Father who continues to provide for me. I see God's hand in my life and can rest in the fact that His love never fails.

God's Healing Presence
Peggy Eastman

How could history be repeating itself in such a cruel way?

The phone call in May 2023 from my sister-in-law, Jill, was a shock, almost as if I had been punched. Again. "Tara is dead," said Jill, as she told me about the sudden death of my nephew Christopher's 38-year-old wife, Tara, from a massive stroke. A wave of grief washed over me, and I could hardly speak or accept the meaning of the words.

In August of 1985 my husband, Jim, had been killed in a plane crash, and this phone call brought it all flooding back, as if I were reliving my own trauma. I was very close to Christopher; he was like the son I had never had. The parallels between us now were eerily similar: I was in my early forties when Jim was killed, and Christopher was forty-one. I was childless when Jim died; Christopher and Tara had no children. I felt Christopher's pain like a heavy weight descending on my chest.

I looked at my favorite photo of Jim; he was smiling broadly. I thought of Tara, so lovely, sweet, and sensitive, so devoted to Christopher. I thought of Christopher, calling emergency services when he found Tara face-down on the floor of their home in California. I thought of the two detectives who had come to my front door in Maryland to break the news of Jim's death in the plane crash in a wooded area of Maine. Tara was young. Why was this sudden-death trauma repeating?

I'd struggled so hard after Jim's death to find God's presence in my desolation. I had joined a bereavement group at my church, stayed in it for 2 years, and found God's presence in my fellow grievers. At the request of our pastor, I had helped our group to write a booklet drawn on God's strength for mourners, "For They Shall Be Comforted." I had joined church Bible study groups and spent hours and hours reading Scripture and praying. I'd written an article for *Guideposts* magazine called "A Widow's Story" to help grieving readers find God in their despair. Was this what it was all for?

> **I will not leave you as orphans; I will come to you.**
>
> —JOHN 14:18 (NIV)

Now, as I sat with the phone in my hand and tears running down my cheeks, I asked God: Were all my years of spiritual preparation leading up to helping Christopher? Was God using me, his aunt who loved him dearly, to step forward and help him start a new, full life? Would I be up to this challenge? Was it my turn to show Christopher how God keeps His promises in comforting the broken-hearted? I was in Maryland and Christopher was in California. I sucked in my breath. I prayed to God that my voice would be strong when I talked to Christopher; I needed to be strong now.

"Christopher," I said over the phone across the miles, "I am so, so sorry about Tara. You were the best husband she could have had." I paused as he gulped and tried to speak. "I have rebuilt my life and so will you," I said firmly. My voice did not waver. "I will do everything I possibly can to help you."

Every morning I started the day by praying for Christopher. *Please, God, help him feel Your loving presence; strengthen him and comfort him. Be with him in his grief and help carry his load. Use me as your channel; flow through me.* I felt God guiding me to help Christopher, almost like a gentle nudge. What I most wanted was for Christopher to know that God would help him go through this tragedy and come out stronger. I didn't want grief to disable him in midlife.

Christopher and I talked on the phone and communicated by email. Mostly, I listened as he talked. I knew all too well about the emotions that come with grief: the flooding rush of sorrow, the arid times of profound loss. I knew how feelings of guilt can emerge during bereavement, even if they are unwarranted—"I should have done more." I knew about the folly of trying to "get back to normal" too quickly. It just wasn't possible.

> **Blessed are those who mourn, for they will be comforted.**
>
> —MATTHEW 5:4 (NIV)

I knew all too well how silent and empty his house must feel without Tara. I knew all about the fear that came in the night, like a rude intruder. I knew what it felt like to dissolve into tears when seeing a sweater or pair of jogging shoes that would never be worn by a beloved spouse again.

"You are not alone," I said. I kept saying it, reassuring Christopher that God was especially close to those who mourn.

I reread what our pastor had told our church bereavement group: "All through life we deal with various losses and forms of grief. But we never seem prepared for the tremendous shocker—the loss of people whose life and personality seem to have been woven into the very fabric of our own existence." The sudden shock: that was the worst. For that kind of shock, only God could provide a lifeline. And He provided it through the people who stepped forward to share the shock and pain.

I told Christopher how much Scripture had meant to me when I lost Jim, precious words that had comforted millions of grievers down through the ages. Quoting John 14:18, I told him that God most especially promises to comfort the broken-hearted and that God always keeps His promises. I desperately wanted my example of moving forward in my life to help Christopher, and I wanted him to share his load of grief on my shoulders.

> **Even though I walk through the valley of the shadow of death, I fear no evil, for you are with me; your rod and your staff, they comfort me.**
>
> —PSALM 23:4 (ESV)

I asked Christopher if he turned to his Bible for comfort when he was in despair, as I had done. "I ordered a new one," he said. "Where shall I start reading?" I was overjoyed; here was an opening to help him grow spiritually. I thought of him holding that big book in his hands; I knew it could be formidable.

"Start with the psalms," I said. "There's a psalm for every human emotion, including sorrow. You will find psalms of comfort and psalms for when you feel rage at God for letting this happen. Whatever you are feeling, there is a psalm to help you. Read them over and over. The more you read them, the more they will help you."

At some future time, I would send Christopher to the book of Job. Job, that good, upright man, lost everything, and still he did not lose his faith in God. Toward the end of his trials, Job says to God, "I know that you can do all things; no purpose of yours can be thwarted" (Job 42:2, NIV). And God restored Job's fortunes and opened to him a good, long life. Tara was gone, but the more I talked to Christopher, the stronger was my sense that God would do the same for him.

Christopher thanked me frequently for my spiritual support. One time when we were talking on the phone, he said, "Thank you for everything, Peggy. You understand." I pictured him sitting in a comfortable stuffed chair, thumbing through the psalms, one of the two cats Tara had rescued and loved nestled on the back of his chair. It was probably Lilah, the black and white one she had found first. *Speak to him, Lord,* I earnestly prayed. *Let Your loving words comfort him and guide him to wholeness. You are the Great Healer.*

As I prayed, I felt a stillness and sense of peace. It was then I knew that God had used me as His channel, a conduit for His healing presence. And I knew in my heart that Christopher would come through this tragedy stronger and closer to his Maker. Spiritually fortified, he would walk in God's light toward his new life.

The Birds
Tanja Dufrene

There was a musky smell in the air as we ascended on creaky steps to the second floor. The antique store was an antique itself, with worn wooden floors and a sagging ceiling. My husband, Donovan, and I were enjoying a day out with our daughter and her three children. The recent weeks had taken their toll on me.

I had finished wandering through the antiques when my daughter reconnected with me, advising a trip to the restroom was needed for her kids. Near the steps going downstairs were two metal chairs. A handwritten note indicated they were not for sale but were placed there for use. So I sat down to await their return.

Welcoming the rest, I observed my surroundings more leisurely. Not often drawn to framed art, I was surprised when a picture caught my eye. The muted earthy tones were inviting. The flattened three-dimensional bird resting on a bent ginkgo branch drew me in. Mesmerized by the beautiful colors and the delicate life forms depicted, my mind quickly wandered through the previous 2 years.

One brief phone call had turned everything upside down. Cancer. Life moved at lightning speed when we learned the prognosis was good, with my treatment expected to end in 6 months. Donovan and I rode a roller coaster of emotions with a whirlwind of medical visits, surgeries, and a new vocabulary to learn.

Fourteen months later I was tired from the long journey. That day, the sky was gray, and the air was cool. The setting matched my mood. Questions remained. Even the doctors were puzzled. I tried not to worry. My emotions ran high, while my energy ran low. Thankfully, my workload was light as I reentered my job from my most recent medical absence. I appreciated the slow transition back in.

Restless and weary, I gazed out the window, longing for spring. A vine wound its way around a trellis. It was bare. The weather was too cold for new growth. I yearned for warmer days and new sprouts, those lovely signs of life and vitality.

Suddenly, a sparrow landed. A robin soon joined it. They bounced from limb to limb, and I was close enough to admire the intricate details of God's design, their earthy colors blending well with the barren branches. Their delicate feathers proved strong as they effortlessly rose with a few flaps of their wings.

This momentary reprieve from life's burdens was refreshing. My days had been filled with a myriad of thoughts troubling

> **Are not two sparrows sold for a penny? Yet not one of them will fall to the ground outside your Father's care. And even the very hairs of your head are all numbered. So don't be afraid; you are worth more than many sparrows.**
>
> —MATTHEW 10:29–31 (NIV)

my soul. *How long would this recovery take? It feels as though I just got back on my feet from the last surgery and navigating the Covid crisis when I was knocked down again. When would the days of pain end? Once my physical body healed, how long until my mind and emotions would feel normal? What would be the result of this medical journey I've been traveling on for well over a year? The cancer had been successfully removed, so why were the physicians puzzled and still seeking a diagnosis?*

The welcome distraction of the fluttering birds ended as they gracefully darted away. Then the Spirit reminded me of Jesus's words in Matthew 10 that we are worth more than many sparrows.

Soon the cold dreary day began to thaw into a heartwarming moment of wonder. God's gentle reminder that I was not forsaken, nor forgotten, breathed fresh air into me. Whatever was happening in my body was not a mystery to Him. My worrying would not restore my health, nor would it bring me peace. It was time to turn my thoughts heavenward. Whatever the days ahead might bring, I was reminded that God has good plans for me.

From that day on, the sight of feathery friends became a comfort to me, a reminder that whatever challenges life presented, I would be cared for. Each speckled feather a sign that God knows every detail.

Now, 2 years later, I held the beautifully crafted artwork depicting a tiny bird on a ginkgo branch, a reminder that my long medical journey had ended. I'd made it through. Now I was healthy, enjoying a place where items of old were signs that better days are coming.

That thought was not lost on me. It was a luxury to visit our daughter because my work schedule did not permit frequent visits. Yet relishing this visit was proving difficult. A few weeks prior, I'd received a cryptic email to meet my boss in

HR. Immediately my heart quickened. My mind raced through previous days and events. I could not identify where I had failed to meet, if not exceed, expectations. *Abba, what is this? Why do I feel threatened? Where is Your peace?* But on that day, there were no speckled birds outside my office window to remind me of His care.

The expression on my boss's face was one I had never seen before. Within moments, the rhythm of my life ended. No longer would I drive to the office every day. No longer would I work with my team. Company leadership had decided to eliminate many positions—including mine.

Instantly, I seemingly transformed from a valued and trusted employee to a potential saboteur. My attitude had not changed, nor had my behavior. I still wanted only the best for my company, my team, and their future. Why did they feel as though I were suddenly a threat? The answer was obvious. I felt threatened; my livelihood had been summarily removed. Of course, it was natural that my employer would have concerns about my response.

> **He gives strength to the weary and increases the power of the weak. . . . But those who hope in the LORD will renew their strength.**
>
> —ISAIAH 40:29–31 (NIV)

Once again I had a torrent of emotions to manage and a desk to clear out. *How can I quietly grab my things and slip away unnoticed like they asked me to? Do my teammates know? Should I say goodbye? How long will it take to find a new job? Where will my next employment be? What will I be doing? How much will I earn? Will it be enough? How much time do we have before we run out of* money? *Abba, where are You? You recently reminded me that my steps are ordered by You. What's the next step?*

At home hours later, I remembered my feathered friends and again found peace, knowing this too would resolve. God had restored health to my body. I had to trust He would lead me to gainful employment.

With my schedule cleared, a visit to our daughter was unexpectedly possible. Now as I sat in the metal chair, the memories and emotions played on the movie screen in my mind. I determined the bird resting on a ginkgo branch would be mine.

Soon my daughter and her littles returned. She discovered items of interest, and we found our way to complete our purchases. As the clerk assisted me, one of the children questioned my selection. I explained that the lovely bird would remind me how God restored my health, and that He would continue to help me through life's challenges.

Eventually, I was offered a position better suited to my skills and interests. The team I joined warmly welcomed me. My commute became twice the distance it had been before, but the warmth of summer was soothing until it became scorching heat because my car's air-conditioning stopped working. Having been unemployed for a third of the year and facing a costly repair such as this was another unwelcome challenge. Fortunately, we found a reliable shop and the repairs were made. Thankfully, my husband was able to work additional hours at his job, so we were able to handle the cost. But shortly after picking up the car we were greeted with another dilemma—the air-conditioning in our house stopped working.

I was desperately trying to persevere, holding on to hope and belief in God's Word, but it became unbearable. My strength and determination dissolved. *God, I don't know how much more I can take!*

Then God lovingly reminded me how to regain fortitude: I must wait in His presence where strength is renewed. While the temperature rose in our home, we were grateful to find it tolerable. We endured ten days without cooling air as our concern grew around our finances. My feathered friend on a ginkgo branch reminded me that God saw, He knew, and longed to help.

Since repairs were too costly, my husband explored options to have the unit replaced. Eventually, the bill came and to our delight, was less than expected. We had withdrawn money from a retirement account, so we used the extra to make additional repairs to our home. The routines of life finally returned, and we continue to revel in the goodness of God.

> **This is what the Sovereign LORD, the Holy One of Israel, says: "In repentance and rest is your salvation, in quietness and trust is your strength, but you would have none of it."**
>
> —ISAIAH 30:15 (NIV)

The gentle reminders of God's love displayed through nature continue to amaze and encourage me. Now a cloudy sky reminds me of His provision when we need cooler days, not when a storm is coming. And a tiny bird flitting through the air or lighting on a branch captures my attention, reminding me that He sees, He knows, and He cares—always.

Lasting Joy
Denise Margaret Ackerman

Everything was going according to plan: My husband, Jim, and I had great jobs, we were settling into our new house, and our first child was due mid-June. I felt like all the best things this world offers were happening in my life, and I was happy.

We had been married just over 3 years when the purchase of our dream home became a reality. The brown-and-white three-bedroom ranch sat nestled on 5 acres of land. We loved all the details of our house, with its open kitchen and hardwood floors. There was a beautiful lawn, majestic willow trees, a cluster of white birch trees shading the welcoming front porch, and a rock garden spilling over with cheerful purple and yellow pansies to greet visitors. Our days were blissfully filled with yardwork, wallpapering, painting, and sprucing up our new home.

Despite a persistent backache, I spent an April day decorating the newly wallpapered nursery and cleaning the house. By evening, I noticed that the pains were coming and going at regular intervals—every 10 minutes. After a frantic phone call to the obstetrician, we immediately began the 30-minute journey to the hospital. My contractions were coming closer and closer together, and I had the overwhelming feeling that Jim should be driving faster.

As soon as we arrived at the labor and delivery ward, Jim was sent to the admitting area to fill out paperwork, while the triage nurse whisked me off to a solitary labor room. She directed me to change into a white and blue–printed hospital gown and then to climb onto the sterile cold bed. My mind raced and my emotions spilled over into tears as the nurse silently adhered electrode pads and lead wires to my tightening tummy to monitor my contractions. She offered no comforting words and seemed unaware of my rising fear. Our baby wasn't due for 2 more months—this could not be happening!

Not long after, our 4-pound, 13-ounce baby boy swiftly made his entrance into our world. There was no time to cradle him in my arms. Instead, our sweet boy was abruptly taken to the small hospital's intensive care unit. By early morning, a special ambulance arrived to transport our little one to the neonatal unit at a large hospital in Syracuse, New York.

> **May the God of hope fill you with all joy and peace as you trust in him, so that you may overflow with hope by the power of the Holy Spirit.**
>
> —ROMANS 15:13 (NIV)

The emptiness I felt at his departure intensified as I watched the other new mothers on the maternity floor take care of their crying babies. Thankfully, my doctor released me the next morning and we made the hour drive to Syracuse to see our son. Peering at him through the glass wall of the NICU was surreal—I felt close to him, yet so very far away. We were not allowed to hold him for the first week. After much deliberation, we chose our son's name, Christopher James Ackerman.

Jim and I were encouraged when Christopher had gained weight and was eating well enough to be moved to a step-down unit. He was ten days old when a nurse mentioned that she thought he might be released in a few days. My mind began to whirl as I thought about how unprepared we were to bring him home. Because Christopher was 2 months early, we hadn't yet bought the newborn outfits, diapers, or baby supplies needed to care for him. My mom and aunt Diane made last-minute plans to host a baby shower for us on the Saturday afternoon of that same week.

On Friday morning, we received a call from the hospital. Christopher had developed some type of mass in his abdomen. On Saturday, the doctors performed explorative surgery and discovered a rare tumor on his liver. Once again, we peered at our son through the glass window of the intensive care unit.

The doctors sent us home, and the dreaded call came shortly after we got there.

Overwhelmed with grief, disappointment, and confusion, I struggled to understand how things could have turned out this way. Throughout Chris's early arrival and gradual improvement, we had prayed for God's help—which we thought was working. But now, instead of celebrating our son with a baby shower that day, we had to plan his funeral. Our perfect world came crashing down. I couldn't imagine ever being happy again. I prayed God would help me through my sorrow, and step by step, He did.

The first moment I sensed God's help was the day of Christopher's funeral. As Jim and I solemnly entered the sanctuary of St. John's Church—the same church where we had exchanged our marriage vows—my eyes were fixed on the tiny white casket covered with a spray of daisies. It was then I heard the Lord whisper to my heart, "Christopher is not here. He is in heaven."

A few weeks after the funeral, Jim and I selected a headstone. We chose the phrase "In His Will Is Our Peace" to be engraved across the top. At the time I did not comprehend what it meant to rely on God's will, yet the statement brought comfort as I longed to experience that peace.

The sorrow and void I experienced over our son's loss drove me to search for hope. As strongly as I believed Christopher was in heaven, I was equally sure I was not qualified to join him there one day. The religious education I received as a child gave me an understanding of sin, heaven, and hell, but lacked assurance of forgiveness or the hope of heaven. I began to search the Bible for answers but had a difficult time making sense of God's Word. I needed someone to teach me how to study.

> **You will seek me and find me when you seek me with all your heart.**
>
> —JEREMIAH 29:13 (NIV)

Over the next few months, God continued to help me by bringing people of faith into my life. As they took the time to share their testimonies with me and answer my questions, I longed for a more meaningful connection to God.

A year after Christopher's death, I yielded my heart and life to the Lord. Coming to a personal faith through Jesus's payment for my sin was the beginning of a life-changing relationship with God. He gave me a brand-new start, overhauling my life's purpose. My selfish quest for happiness gradually was replaced with a desire to live my life to please God. His presence began to pour into the empty areas of my heart, easing the hurt that had overtaken it.

God knew I still had much to learn about His plan for my life and that I needed help understanding His Word. Jane, one of the faithful friends who God had given me as an encouragement during my season of grief, introduced me to Kay, a young mother from my town. Kay offered to meet with me to study the Bible. I was amazed that someone I didn't know would be willing to put so much effort into helping me, Kay became a spiritual mentor who helped lead me closer to God.

> I have told you this so that my joy may be in you and that your joy may be complete.
>
> —JOHN 15:11 (NIV)

Once a week for the next 20 weeks, Kay sat at my kitchen table with her Bible opened, patiently guiding me as I slowly thumbed my way through the New and Old Testaments, searching through chapters and verses that strengthened me in my quest for hope. Kay lovingly explained the fundamental truths of God's Word to me. I learned that God is a loving Father who created me for a purpose, that Jesus was His earthly image, and that God sent the Holy Spirit to strengthen and guide me.

As I began to learn more about the Lord, my faith was strengthened. Growing closer to Him gave me a strong foundation that was not built on emotion but rather on the truths found in the Bible. I began to personally experience God's love for me and gradually started to trust Him with my life. Kay taught me by her example of investing in my spiritual growth that our purpose as believers is to share with others what the Lord has done for us.

GOD'S GIFT OF TASTE
— Linda L. Kruschke —

POTATOES PROVIDE A versatile staple in many cultures. Though the flavor of potatoes on their own can be bland and uninspiring, there are a myriad of potato recipes that delight the taste buds, such as potatoes au gratin, baked potatoes with all the toppings, or simple hash browns with a little salt and pepper.

Like the potato, the Word of God can be accessed and enjoyed in a myriad of ways. Trying a new approach—such as studying it in a group, listening to audio recordings, or reading it with prayerful intention—can give words that might seem ordinary a whole new flavor.

Spending time in God's Word filled my heart with joy. The loss I had experienced was softened with hope, as I gained the assurance that one day I would be reunited with Christopher in heaven. My joy has been tested and remained steadfast over the years as I went through three additional (and very complicated) pregnancies. The Lord generously blessed us with a beautiful daughter, amazing twin sons, and another baby who joined Chris in heaven.

Whether I am facing a season of heartache and trial or a season of ease and blessing, my faith in God upholds me. His presence is the calming strength that brings lasting joy that is not based on circumstances. I am so thankful God faithfully led me through each step in my journey to find joy in Him.

Contributors

Denise Margaret Ackerman   p. 224
Sandra G. Beck   p. 94
Rhoda Blecker   p. 163
Bettie Boswell   pp. 14, 105
Tez Brooks   p. 154
Elsa Kok Colopy   p. 81
Laurie Davies   p. 174
Debbie Dueck   p. 74
Tanja Dufrene   p. 218
Peggy Eastman   p. 213
Susan Engebrecht   p. 198
Elizabeth Erlandson   p. 41
Valorie Bridges Fant   p. 143
Joyce Farinella   p. 18
Heidi Gaul   p. 194
Tina Savant Gibson   p. 89
Felicia Harris-Russell   p. 85
Lynne Hartke   pp. 39, 68
Kim Taylor Henry   pp. 93, 166
Laurie Herlich   p. 54
Becky Hofstad   p. 99
Pamela Horton   p. 131
Leanne Jackson   p. 186

Heather Jepsen   p. 158
Tara Johnson   p. 112
Ashley Kappel   p. 204
Angela J. Kaufman   p. 24
Linda L. Kruschke   pp. 98, 229
Kathryn C. Lang   p. 125
Lisa Lenning   p. 48
Brenda Glanzer Lilliston   p. 24
Louis Lotz   p. 4
Cynthia A. Lovely   p. 36
Allison Lynn   p. 149
Eryn Lynum   pp. 46, 142
Rachel M. Mathew   p. 137
Roberta Messner   p. 180
Marsha H. Myers   p. 168
Sandra Kirby Quandt   p. 60
Linda J. Reeves   p. 118
Kimberly Shumate   pp. 23, 72
Susan Dietz Shumway   p. 208
Buck Storm   p. 212
Stacey Thureen   p. 190
Terrie Todd   p. 185
Poppy Webb   p. 29

Acknowledgments

Every attempt has been made to credit the sources of copyrighted material used in this book. If any such acknowledgment has been inadvertently omitted or miscredited, receipt of such information would be appreciated.

Scripture quotations marked (ESV) are taken from the *Holy Bible, English Standard Version*. Copyright © 2001 by Crossway Bibles, a division of Good News Publishers. Used by permission. All rights reserved.

Scripture quotations marked (JPS) are taken from *Tanakh: A New Translation of the Holy Scriptures according to the Traditional Hebrew Text*. Copyright © 1985 by the Jewish Publication Society. All rights reserved.

Scripture quotations marked (KJV) are taken from the *King James Version of the Bible*.

Scripture quotations marked (NASB) or (NASB1995) are taken from the *New American Standard Bible*®, Copyright © 1960, 1971, 1977, 1995, 2020 by The Lockman Foundation. All rights reserved.

Scripture quotations marked (NIRV) are taken from the *Holy Bible*, *New International Reader's Version*. Copyright © 1995, 1996, 1998, 2014 by Biblica, Inc. Used by permission. All rights reserved worldwide.

Scripture quotations marked (NIV) are taken from *The Holy Bible*, *New International Version*. Copyright © 1973, 1978, 1984, 2011 by Biblica, Inc. Used by permission of Zondervan. All rights reserved worldwide. zondervan.com

Scripture quotations marked (NKJV) are taken from *The Holy Bible, New King James Version*. Copyright © 1982 by Thomas Nelson.

Scripture quotations marked (NLT) are taken from *Holy Bible, New Living Translation*. Copyright © 1996, 2004, 2007 by Tyndale House Foundation. Used by permission of Tyndale House Publishers Inc., Carol Stream, Illinois. All rights reserved.

Scripture quotations marked (NRSVUE) are taken from the *New Revised Standard Version, Updated Edition*. Copyright © 2021 National Council of Churches of Christ in the United States of America. Used by permission. All rights reserved worldwide.

A Note from the Editors

We hope you enjoyed *Embraced by His Light*, published by Guideposts. For over 75 years, Guideposts, a nonprofit organization, has been driven by a vision of a world filled with hope. We aspire to be the voice of a trusted friend, a friend who makes you feel more hopeful and connected.

By making a purchase from Guideposts, you join our community in touching millions of lives, inspiring them to believe that all things are possible through faith, hope, and prayer. Your continued support allows us to provide uplifting resources to those in need. Whether through our communities, websites, apps, or publications, we inspire our audiences, bring them together, and comfort, uplift, entertain, and guide them. Visit us at guideposts.org to learn more.

We would love to hear from you. Write us at Guideposts, P.O. Box 5815, Harlan, Iowa 51593 or call us at (800) 932-2145. Did you love *Embraced by His Light*? Leave a review for this product on guideposts.org/shop. Your feedback helps others in our community find relevant products.

Find inspiration, find faith, find Guideposts.

Shop our best sellers and favorites at
guideposts.org/shop
Or scan the QR code to go directly to our Shop